BY REQUEST
Highlights

The Search for Hawai'i's Greatest Recipes Continues

Betty Shimabukuro

All photos by Betty Shimabukuro unless otherwise noted below:
Courtesy of the Royal Hawaiian: pg. 178
Photos © The *Honolulu Star-Advertiser*:
   pg. 78, 86, 172 by staff; background photo pg. viii-27 by Anna Pacheco; pg. 4, 70 by Cindy Ellen Russell, pg. 12 by Krystle Marcellus; pg. 21, 54, 64, 74, 103, 160 by George F. Lee; pg. 24, 26, 27 by Jamm Aquino; pg. 28 (top), 32, 33, 35, 52 (top), 61, 68, 76 (bottom), 94, 100, 154 by Dennis Oda; pg. 28 (bottom), 38 by Kevin German; pg. 30, 52 (bottom), 56, 164 by Craig T. Kojima; pg. 42, 136, 158, 159 by F.L. Morris; pg. 82 by Dean Sensui; pg. 106 by Ken Sakamoto
Spot photography from dreamstime.com:
   pg. i ©Masyaka; background photo pg. ii-vii, 184-189 ©Hawkeye978; pg. iv, vi, 2, 7, 29, 39, 59, 109, 157, 166, 174, 177 ©Conceptcafe; cutting board pg. vii, 1, 29, 53, 77, 109, 135, 157 ©Ivantocovlad; pg. 22 © Ilyach; background photo pg. 28-51 ©Yotka; pg. 40 ©Lapuma; pg. 46©Lemuana; background photo pg. 52-75, pg. 76-107 ©Mustipan; pg. 53 ©Alexanderpokusay; pg. 62, 128 ©Krisdog; pg. 77 ©Mozart3737; pg. 85, 98, 118 ©Epineart; pg. 96 ©Marinavorontsova; pg. 107 ©Setory; background photo pg. 108-133 ©Nilsz; background photo pg. 134-155 ©Udra11; pg. 135 ©Oleksandraklymenko; background photo pg. 156-183 ©Szefei

ISBN-13: 978-1939487-80-3
Library of Congress Control Number: 2017908294

Design by Jane Gillespie
First Printing, September 2017
Second Printing, August 2018

Mutual Publishing, LLC
1215 Center Street, Suite 210
Honolulu, Hawai'i 96816
Ph: (808) 732-1709
Fax: (808) 734-4094
e-mail: info@mutualpublishing.com
www.mutualpublishing.com

Printed in South Korea

CONTENTS

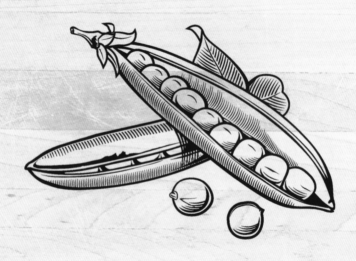

INTRODUCTION

When I inherited the "By Request" column, I also inherited a stack of letters. Words written on paper, all from people looking for recipes. It was 1998 and "By Request" already had been running in the *Honolulu Star-Bulletin* for years.

These days I rarely receive a request via the postal service or even by phone; almost everything comes by email. That same online connection means that readers can now find a lot of what they need from the vast information pool known as the internet.

If I were to define the continuing mission of "By Request," I'd say it is to boldly go where Google has not gone before.

I still get requests for recipes from restaurants that closed decades ago, for long-gone school cafeteria favorites, and for those rare recipes that just can't be found online. In that regard I haven't quite outlived my usefulness.

"By Request" continued through the 2010 merger of the *Honolulu Star-Bulletin* and the *Honolulu Advertiser*, and marches on in *Crave*, the weekly food magazine launched by the *Star-Advertiser* in 2016. Much has changed, but at its core "By Request" still aims to connect those who love to cook with great, time-tested recipes.

The first edition of the "By Request" cookbook was published in 2006; a second in 2010. Both are now out of print. This book dips back into the previous books for highlights, and adds some new favorites.

My hope is that you will open this book and find something you've just gotta try. Then, get out a knife. Turn on the stove. Begin.

Happy cooking!

punahou beef stew

we'll have two forks please

kapalama school peanut butter coffee cake

SCHOOL LUNCH

Some day someone is going to publish a cookbook of recipes from Hawai'i's public schools. That person is going to become a superhero. And perhaps a millionaire.

You think I exaggerate, but you have not been reading my mail.

Many, many, many people are nostalgic for the foods of the school cafeteria, from the 1950s through the 1980s. Some insist they can remember the exact taste of an old favorite—it's stuck firmly in the place where memory intersects with the taste buds.

Why? I can only guess.

Perhaps because the meals connect to youth and good times. Perhaps because the meals were a departure from what was served at home. Perhaps some of those cafeteria managers just knew what kids would like.

My theory: It's the butter and the American cheese.

Both these items were federal government surplus, or "commodity foods," given to the schools in quantity.

You'll notice that many of the recipes here are for cookies, as these are particular reader favorites. Why? I say it's the butter. A generation ago butter may have been a luxury in the home, but schools had it by the caseload. No wonder the cookies seemed so fabulous.

You'll also notice that many of the favorite savory dishes are layered in American cheese. It's a key flavor profile from that era.

Tracking down those older recipes can be difficult, as many favorite dishes are no longer in the DOE menu rotation and the recipes were the purview of particular cafeteria managers who by now are long retired.

Over the years I've gotten lucky a few times, yielding the collection of recipes in this section. I only wish it were larger.

When I was in school this dish was called baked spaghetti—the pasta and sauce all familiar, but the form more solid than any respectable Italian spaghetti.

This is the version served at Lunalilo Elementary School, and the secret appears to be the addition of quite a bit of American cheese, which kids like and which boosts the protein content.

Once cooked, the sauce is mixed in with the cooked pasta and the pans are put under 200-degree warmers and held until lunchtime. The noodles absorb a lot of the sauce, making the dish quite firm—in fact, you can cut it like lasagna.

To recreate this effect at home, place your pan in a warm oven.

LUNALILO SCHOOL SPAGHETTI
Serves 10

1 pound ground beef
3 tablespoons dehydrated onions
2 (1½-ounce) packages spaghetti sauce mix (McCormick brand preferred)
Pepper to taste
½ teaspoon dried oregano
1 teaspoon granulated garlic
5 cups crushed tomatoes
1½ tablespoons chicken base (see note)
½ to 1 teaspoon Worcestershire sauce
¾ teaspoon sugar, or more to taste
Salt to taste
10 ounces (13 slices) American cheese
1 pound uncooked spaghetti

Brown ground beef. Drain fat; add onions, spaghetti sauce mix, pepper, oregano and garlic. Stir in tomatoes, chicken base, Worcestershire sauce, sugar, and salt. Bring to a boil; reduce heat and simmer 45 minutes.

Meanwhile cook spaghetti. Drain, but do not rinse.

Stir cheese into sauce to melt then stir in spaghetti.

Transfer pasta and sauce to a baking pan and cover with foil. Place in a 200°F oven for 1 hour.

Note: Chicken base is a paste, sold in supermarkets alongside chicken broth or bouillon.

Turkey Corn Scallop is a relative of Turkey Ala King or Chicken Ala King, a comforting dish with a creamy sauce.

The word "scallop" in the name refers not to seafood but to the addition of potatoes, as this dish is also a little like scalloped potatoes.

This version comes from Darryl Okamura, cafeteria manager at Kaiser High School, who says he first made it at Iliahi Elementary School in Wahiawā.

If you're old enough and went to public school in Hawai'i, the taste will take you back. The key is American cheese, melted into the dish at the very end. "Makes it yummy," Okamura says.

Turn this into Turkey Ala King by eliminating the potatoes and trading out the corn for bell peppers, peas, carrots, and/or mushrooms.

TURKEY CORN SCALLOP
Serves 8

2 cups water
1 large potato, diced (about 2 cups)
2 pounds diced cooked turkey
1 (15-ounce) can corn, with liquid
2 tablespoons diced onion
2 tablespoons chicken base (see note)
2 cups whole milk
¼ cup cornstarch dissolved in ¼ cup water
8 slices American cheese, cut in small pieces
Salt and pepper, to taste

Bring water to boil in large pot. Add potatoes, reduce heat and simmer until potatoes can be pierced with a fork but are still firm, about 5 minutes. Do not drain. Add turkey, corn (with liquid) and onion to pot with potatoes.

Combine chicken base with a small amount of milk, stirring until smooth. Add to pot with remaining milk. Add more water if needed just so mixture is covered in liquid. Simmer over medium heat until hot.

Gradually stir in cornstarch mixture until thickened (you might not need it all). Add cheese and stir until melted. Taste; add salt and pepper as needed.

Note: Chicken base is a paste, sold in supermarkets alongside chicken broth or bouillon.

Ah, Spanish rice. I remember you well. You followed me from elementary school in Hilo through high school in Hawai'i Kai, a staple of cafeterias statewide.

And I am not alone. Most of my fellow public-school alumni remember this dish, some unkindly, but most with some degree of reverence.

Marlow DeRego, a retired cafeteria manager and Leeward District supervisor for DOE food service, helped me with this recipe and some context.

First, most cookbook recipes for Spanish rice call for cooking raw rice in a soupy mixture of tomatoes and ground beef. Most schools, DeRego said, have giant rice steamers, so they'd cook the rice and sauce separately, then mix them in a baking pan.

But alas: "Schools discontinued Spanish rice due to USDA regulatory changes to requirements to meet grain, protein, and vegetable portions," DeRego said. "Hence, this dish is now a memory!"

If this recipe doesn't quite match your taste memory, that's probably because your cafeteria manager tweaked the recipe. Try adding granulated garlic or garlic salt, chili powder or a little tomato paste.

SCHOOL-KINE SPANISH RICE

Adapted from Hilo Union School

Serves 6

2 tablespoons vegetable oil

1 cup diced onion

1 pound lean ground beef

1 cup diced green bell pepper

1 cup diced celery

2 (14-ounce) cans stewed tomatoes, crushed, or 1 can stewed
tomatoes and 1 can condensed tomato soup

½ teaspoon salt

¼ teaspoon pepper

2 cups cooked rice (white, brown, or a mix)

4 slices American cheese, cut in strips

Heat oil in large skillet over medium-high. Add onion; sauté until softened. Add beef; sauté until nearly cooked through. Add bell pepper, celery, tomatoes, salt, and pepper. Reduce heat and simmer, covered, 5 to 10 minutes, until vegetables are tender.

Heat oven to 350°F. Combine sauce and rice in a casserole dish or baking pan. Top with cheese. Bake a few minutes, until cheese melts.

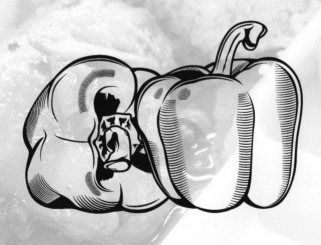

Ground beef and green beans are the basis of another cafeteria favorite: Spanish Green Beans, although I really don't see where the "Spanish" comes in. It's another dish no longer on school menus—a simple mix of ground beef, onions, and garlic simmered in a light tomato sauce with canned green beans. The official DOE version, based on the dish as once served at August Ahrens Elementary School in Waipahu, uses quite a bit of celery and ground cumin.

SPANISH GREEN BEANS
Adapted from August Ahrens Elementary School
Serves 6

2 tablespoons vegetable oil
1 onion, diced (about 2 cups)
3 garlic cloves, minced
3 celery stalks, diced (OK to include leaves)
1 pound lean ground beef
½ teaspoon salt (or more, to taste)
¼ teaspoon black pepper
1 heaping teaspoon ground cumin
1 (15-ounce) can tomato sauce or 1 ounce tomato paste
1¾ cups water (fill up the tomato sauce can)
2 (14.5-ounce) cans green beans, drained
1 tablespoon flour dissolved in 1 tablespoon water

Heat oil in large skillet over medium-high. Add onions, garlic, and celery; sauté until softened. Add ground beef with salt, pepper, and cumin. Sauté until meat is browned.

Add tomato sauce and water; simmer 30 minutes.

Stir in beans. Drizzle in flour-water mixture. Simmer another 5 minutes to thicken. Taste and adjust seasonings.

Reney Ching, head cook at Punahou School, contributed two recipes for stews—one chicken and one beef—that she says are favorites with students.

The chicken stew has been on the menu at least since the eighties, appearing every six weeks in the meal rotation. "The kids love this," Ching said. "I love it. Very comfort food."

It has peas, carrots, and potatoes in a gravy of ginger-flavored chicken broth thickened with a margarine-flour roux. It's the ginger and the roux that elevate the dish from a pot of chicken to a very satisfying stew. ("Roux" may be intimidating, sounding so French and all, but in this case it just means beating margarine and flour until creamy.)

The result might remind you of a good chicken pot pie—without the pie.

For the beef stew, Ching, credits her grandmother with the basic technique. She'd always make a beef broth first, simmering the meat in water with a bit of salt, then she'd turn that broth into a gravy and add vegetables. All the while the meat would be simmering its way to tenderness.

PUNAHOU BEEF STEW
Serves 10

4 cups water
5 pounds boneless beef short ribs or chuck roast, cut in bite-size cubes, rinsed
1 teaspoon salt
4 tablespoons (4 large cubes) beef bouillon
2 tablespoons chopped garlic
2 (8 ounce) cans tomato sauce
¼ cup cornstarch, dissolved in ¼ cup water
3 large red potatoes, peeled and cut in large pieces (don't cut pieces too small or they will disintegrate while cooking)
16 ounces pearl onions, peeled (see note)
2 cups diced carrots
1 cup diced celery

Bring water to boil; add beef and salt. Cover and simmer over medium heat 1 hour. Meat will be cooked through but might be tough. Do not be alarmed.

Add bouillon, garlic, and tomato sauce. Cover and simmer until meat is tender, about 30 minutes for short ribs, up to 1 hour for chuck roast.

Add cornstarch mixture gradually, stirring to thicken sauce to desired consistency (you may not need all the cornstarch).

Add potatoes, onions, carrots, and celery; simmer another 20 to 30 minutes until potatoes and carrots are tender.

Note: Fresh pearl onions can be found in bags near the onions in the produce section of supermarkets. To save having to peel, buy frozen onions and add in last 10 minutes of cooking time. Or substitute a large regular onion, cut in wedges.

PUNAHOU CHICKEN STEW
Serves 6

3 pounds boneless, skinless chicken thighs
1 (2-inch) piece ginger, smashed
½ tablespoon sea salt or kosher salt
6 tablespoons margarine, melted
5 to 6 tablespoons flour
8 large cloves garlic, minced
¼ teaspoon white pepper
½ teaspoon nutmeg
1 pound white potatoes, peeled and diced (about 3 cups)
1 pound frozen peas and carrots

Place chicken in pot and cover with water (2 to 3 cups). Add ginger and salt. Bring to boil, then lower heat and simmer until cooked through, about 30 minutes. Skim fat and oil while cooking. Remove chicken; discard ginger. Keep broth simmering.

Make roux by beating margarine and flour using an electric mixer. Add flour gradually, beating until roux is thick and creamy (you might not need all the flour). Slowly add roux to simmering broth, stirring until thickened (you might not need all the roux). Stir in garlic, pepper, nutmeg, and potatoes.

Cut chicken into bite-size pieces and return to pot. Cover and simmer until potatoes are cooked, about 15 minutes.

Add peas and carrots and simmer until heated through.

This recipe originated at Iliahi Elementary School in Wahiawā, the first public school posting of Darryl Okamura, who is now cafeteria manager at my alma mater, Kaiser High School.

"I keep all the recipes from the schools I worked at," he said. "The sweet rolls from that school are the best."

His recipe was for 200 buns, so this is a reduced version and might not exactly match what's served in the cafeteria. But I made a batch, and the rolls were remarkably good, soft, slightly sweet, with a hint of lemon that makes them distinctive.

ILIAHI ELEMENTARY
PORTUGUESE SWEET ROLLS
Makes about 40 rolls

18.5 ounces (about 3½ cups) bread flour
½ teaspoon salt
3 tablespoons plus 1 teaspoon powdered milk (see note)
4 ounces (about ½ cup) sugar
2 tablespoons rapid-rise yeast
¼ cup unsalted butter, softened
1 egg
1½ cups warm water (120°F to 130°F)
1 tablespoon plus 1 teaspoon lemon extract

Line a cookie sheet or sheet pan with baking parchment.

Sift together flour, salt, powdered milk, and sugar. Stir in yeast and butter, until butter is distributed. Add egg, then warm water and extract. Mix, using bread hook in a standing mixer, or stir by hand until dough is smooth (may be sticky).

Roll dough into walnut-size balls on prepared cookie sheet. If dough is too soft to handle, spoon it out, or sprinkle in a little more flour (not too much or texture of rolls will be affected). Let rise until doubled in size, 60 to 90 minutes.

Heat oven to 350°F (325°F for a convection oven).

Bake rolls 20 minutes, or until light brown.

Note: Powdered milk can be replaced by 1½ cups warm whole milk. Eliminate water from recipe.

This baked goodie came not from the cafeteria but from a home economics class at McKinley High School in the 1980s. It's distinctive because unlike most thin, crunchy lavash, this one is a bit thicker and has some "chew."

Lavash traditionally has no leavener, such as baking soda, or eggs, but this recipe has both, undoubtedly contributing to the texture. You can control the relative crunchiness by adjusting the thickness as you roll it out. I rolled mine out to less than 1/8-inch thickness, but it baked up to about ¼-inch. One batch was like a cracker in texture; the other, baked a shorter time, was chewier.

A suggestion: Since you roll the dough in four separate pieces, bake the first one as a test. Let it cool and break off a piece to taste. If you want a crunchier or chewier end result, roll out the rest of the dough accordingly, and adjust baking time.

MCKINLEY HIGH SCHOOL LAVASH
Serves 8 to 10

3¼ cups flour
½ cup sugar
½ teaspoon salt
½ teaspoon baking soda
2 tablespoons sesame seeds
½ cup (1 stick) margarine
1 egg, slightly beaten
²/₃ cup milk

Heat oven to 350°F. Combine flour, sugar, salt, and baking soda. Add sesame seeds. Cut in margarine until mixture is crumbly.

Combine egg and milk; add to flour mixture. Divide dough into 4 parts.

Roll 1 part out very thin on floured surface (form a rough rectangle at least 10 inches across). Loosen immediately and place on ungreased cookie sheet (dough can be rolled around the rolling pin and lifted, as you would a pie crust). Bake about 30 minutes, until golden brown and firm. Transfer to rack to cool (it will get crisper as it cools). Break into pieces.

Repeat with remaining 3 parts of dough.

Note: You could sprinkle rolled out dough with more sesame seeds, then roll again to press seeds in. Transfer to cookie sheet. This was not part of the McKinley recipe, but is an option that makes the lavash look nicer.

We never had peanut butter coffee cake in any of the school cafeterias in any of the institutions of my public school career. I want my money back.

The recipe was volunteered by Jade Tom, the baker at Kapalama Elementary from 2000 to 2006. It is delicious. Like a peanut butter cookie in a soft cake form.

Note that Tom gives ingredient measurements by weight. This is the most precise way to tackle the recipe, but for those who don't have scales, I have added approximate volume measurements.

KAPALAMA SCHOOL
PEANUT BUTTER COFFEE CAKE
Makes a 13 x 9-inch cake

½ pound (2 sticks) butter
1¼ pounds (about 2½ cups) sugar
1 pound 4 ounces (about 2½ cups) peanut butter
3 large eggs
1 pound 2 ounces (about 3½ cups) flour
1¼ tablespoons baking powder
1 teaspoon salt
½ cup powdered milk
2 cups water
1 cup raisins, optional

Topping
½ cup sugar
¼ cup flour
2 tablespoons butter
½ teaspoon cinnamon

Heat oven to 325°F. Grease two 8- or 9-inch square baking pans. Cream butter with sugar, then beat in peanut butter and eggs.

Sift together flour, baking powder, and salt. Stir in powdered milk. Add to peanut butter mixture, alternating with water. Batter will be thick but should not be chunky (if so, add more water). Fold in raisins, if using. Spread in pans.

To make topping: Cut sugar and flour into butter until crumbly. Sprinkle with cinnamon and mix. Spread over top of cake; press down lightly. Bake about 1 hour, until a pick inserted in center comes out clean.

Note: Rather than buy a box of powdered milk to get just ½ cup, I used 2 cups of milk in place of the water.

As a longtime volunteer for various school groups (three kids—that's a LOT of school carnivals), I know well the value of a parent with specialized skills who is willing to donate them to the cause. So I salute the anonymous cafeteria manager who gives his cookie-baking talent to Roosevelt High School's Project Graduation.

His Frosted Flake Chocolate Chip Cookies have been all the rage at several of the group's fundraisers.

FROSTED FLAKE
CHOCOLATE CHIP COOKIES
Makes about 2 dozen

4 cups Frosted Flakes
2 sticks (1 cup) butter
¾ cup sugar
1 teaspoon vanilla
2 cups flour
1 teaspoon baking soda
½ cup chocolate chips

Heat oven to 325°F. Line a cookie sheet with parchment.

Crush Frosted Flakes lightly (until they compress to about 3 cups; don't make them too fine).

Cream butter and sugar until fluffy. Add vanilla.

Combine flour and baking soda; gradually add to butter mixture and stir to combine. Fold in crushed Frosted Flakes and chocolate chips. Mixture will be crumbly. It's best to use your hands to make sure ingredients combine evenly. Roll 2-tablespoon portions of dough into balls and place on cookie sheet. Flatten slightly.

Bake about 20 minutes, until lightly brown. Cookies will be soft but will firm up as they cool. Don't over bake or cookies will become very hard.

Peanut butter cookies have not been served in schools for a decade due to peanut allergies among students. Score one for the good old days.

This recipe was adapted from one used at 'Ānuenue Elementary, but I baked up a batch and was immediately transported back to Niu Valley Intermediate School.

'ĀNUENUE ELEMENTARY SCHOOL
PEANUT BUTTER COOKIES
Makes about 6 dozen

1 cup butter or shortening
1 cup white sugar
1 cup brown sugar
1 egg, well beaten
1 cup creamy peanut butter
1 teaspoon vanilla
2 cups flour
1 teaspoon baking soda
½ teaspoon salt

Heat oven to 350°F.

In large mixing bowl, cream butter and sugars. Add egg, peanut butter, and vanilla; blend well.

Sift together flour, baking soda, and salt. Add to creamed mixture; blend well.

Shape into walnut-size balls and place on baking sheet lined with parchment paper. Flatten with fork to about ¼-inch thickness. Bake 12 to 15 minutes until golden brown.

Cafeteria shortbread cookies were simply the best. Many of my readers remember volunteering for cafeteria duty because they'd get extra.

I remember roving bands of boys at my school who would swipe the precious bars off plates. Thugs. I once threatened one of them with a fork. Edith Ichimasa, retired cafeteria manager from Kailua High School, still has the cookie recipe used throughout her tenure. The key to the cookie's deliciousness: loads of butter.

Shortbread was baked nearly every day at the high school, Ichimasa said, and they kept several 5-gallon cans full. Cookies were sold as an add-on to the 25-cent daily lunch, four for a dime. Sometimes they added nuts, she said, but the kids preferred their shortbread plain.

Years after her retirement, Ichimasa's former students still carry a torch for those cookies. "I was in the hospital and one of the nurses recognized me. She asked if I ever share the recipe."

Yes, she does.

KAILUA HIGH SCHOOL
SHORTBREAD COOKIES
Makes about 2 dozen

2 sticks (1 cup) butter
½ cup sugar
2⅓ cups sifted flour
¼ teaspoon salt

Heat oven to 300°F. Grease a 9-inch square baking pan or line with baking parchment.

Cream butter. Gradually add sugar and beat until light and fluffy. Work in flour and salt with fingertips until well combined and crumbly. Press evenly into baking pan. Prick all over with fork. Bake 50 to 60 minutes, until golden brown. Cool slightly, then cut into bars.

Enter today's heroine, Gaylynn Kalama, retired 'Aikahi Elementary School custodian, who found this recipe in a cookbook that the school's parents and staff put out in the 1980s. It was contributed by cafeteria manager Suanne Miyata, who retired last year. "This cookie is wonderfully buttery and chocolatey, still talked about till this day," Kalama wrote.

'AIKAHI CHOCOLATE
SHORTBREAD COOKIES
Makes about 3 dozen

⅓ cup unsweetened cocoa powder
¼ cup hot water
2 sticks (1 cup) butter
1⅓ cups sugar
½ teaspoon vanilla
2½ cups flour, sifted

Heat oven to 350°F. Line a cookie sheet with baking parchment.

Dissolve cocoa in hot water, stirring until smooth.

Cream butter and sugar until fluffy. Add vanilla. Gradually mix in half the flour. Add cocoa, then gradually add remaining flour. Dough should be firm but not so dry that it becomes difficult to mix. You may not need all the flour.

Form dough into 1½-inch balls and place on cookie sheet. Bake about 20 minutes (cookies should barely hold an indentation when you press them with a finger). Cool on rack.

Note: For a crunchier cookie, do not dissolve cocoa powder in water. Reduce the amount of flour by ¼ to ½ cup, adding it gradually, according to the instructions. Be careful not to overbake. This recipe can be doubled but, again, be very careful about the flour.

This recipe was donated anonymously by 1959 graduate of Kahuku High School and a member of the Future Homemakers of America. The group's adviser was Miss Fukumitsu, the school's cafeteria manager, who gave the young bakers a recipe for a school favorite—cherry crisp.

This dessert is a winner: sweet, tart, soft, crunchy, and very buttery, all at once.

The crucial ingredient is canned tart cherries—not the same as more expensive and harder-to-find cherry pie filling. Look for them in the canned fruit aisle, not the baking aisle; a common brand is Oregon Fruit Products. I get mine at Walmart.

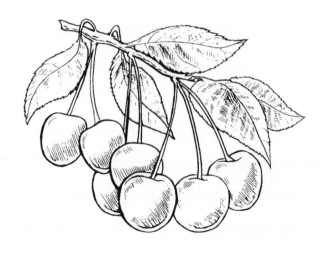

KAHUKU HIGH SCHOOL
CHERRY CRISP

Crust
2½ cups flour
¼ cup sugar
1 cup butter, cold and cut into cubes

Filling
3 (14.5-ounce) cans (about 4 cups) tart cherries, drained
1 teaspoon cinnamon
1½ cups sugar
¼ teaspoon salt
3 tablespoons cornstarch

Heat oven to 450°F. Grease a 13 x 9-inch pan.

For crust, combine flour and sugar. Cut in cold butter until pea-size pieces of dough form. Spread half of mixture into bottom of pan and press down gently. Do not pack. Bake 10 minutes, until lightly brown. Reduce heat to 350°F.

Combine filling ingredients. Spread over crust and top with remaining crust mixture. Bake 30 to 40 minutes, until top is browned. Will be quite soft when warm; firmer when chilled.

Kathie Young collected this trio of cookie recipes in the 1970s when her children attended, and she was a volunteer at, Haha'ione Elementary School.

The cookies are all familiar, but with a twist: oatmeal cookies with ground raisins that provide a special moistness and flavor; a light, delicate shortbread called Grandmother Cookies; and brownies made with peanut butter that turn out wonderfully chewy. Those brownies were known at other schools as Peanut Butter Chews.

Young is a self-described cookie monster. "I would sit around all day long eating cookies if I had them," she says.

Haha'ione did not have its own kitchen forty years ago, so meals were brought in from another school. But when Young asked for recipes, one of the cafeteria workers came through.

"I think they just gave me a bunch of papers with a bajillion cookies on them," she recalls.

The quantities were huge, the recipes lacked instructions, and the ingredient lists called for such things as powdered eggs, but Young and her husband did the math and made the ingredient conversions.

The cookies became family favorites, "my Christmas gifts when we didn't have any money."

PEANUT BUTTER BROWNIES
AKA PEANUT BUTTER CHEWS
Makes about 3 dozen

¼ cup butter
2 cups sugar
1¾ cups unpacked brown sugar
5 eggs
1⅓ cups peanut butter
1½ teaspoons vanilla
3 cups flour
1½ teaspoons baking powder
1 teaspoon salt

Heat oven to 350°F. Lightly grease a 9 x 13-inch cake pan.

Cream butter and sugars. Beat in eggs, 1 at a time, then peanut butter and vanilla.

Combine flour, baking powder, and salt; add gradually to peanut butter mixture. Batter may be stiff. Spread evenly in pan and bake 25 to 30 minutes.

Cool, then cut into squares, or use cookie cutters to cut into shapes.

Variation: Fold ½ cup chocolate chips into batter or press into top of batter before baking.

ROLLED OATS AND RAISIN COOKIES
Makes 4 dozen

1½ cups butter
¾ cup sugar
6 tablespoons lightly packed brown sugar
⅔ cup ground raisins (see note)
2½ teaspoons vanilla
1 tablespoon vegetable oil
3½ cups flour
1¾ teaspoons baking soda
2¼ cups rolled oats

Heat oven to 400°F.

Cream butter and sugars. Beat in ground raisins, then vanilla and oil.

Combine flour, baking soda, and rolled oats. Gradually add to butter mixture, mixing until well combined.

Form into 1½ inch balls (if batter is dry add a little more oil). Place 2 inches apart on cookie sheets and bake 12 minutes.

Note: Grind raisins in a food processor into a sticky mass, or mince finely with a knife.

Variation: For loaded oatmeal cookies, add chocolate chips, chopped nuts, and/or shredded coconut—a total of about 1½ cups of add-ins.

GRANDMOTHER COOKIES

Makes 4 dozen

1½ cups sugar
¾ cup butter
1¼ cups vegetable shortening
2¾ teaspoons vanilla
4 cups flour
2 teaspoons baking soda

Heat oven to 350°F.

Cream sugar, butter, and shortening. Add vanilla.

Combine flour and baking soda. Add gradually to sugar mixture, mixing until combined. Form batter into 1½ inch balls and place on cookie sheets about 2 inches apart.

Flatten with glass dipped in sugar. Bake 15 to 20 minutes.

Variation: Add 2 cups slightly crushed cornflakes to batter.

chef dennis franks

paul chun's pancakes

THE BREAKFAST CLUB

We should pay more attention to breakfast, given its importance in getting the day started right. Yes, mornings are rushed and sometimes it's all we can do to hit the road on time with a piece of toast in hand.

What I'm offering here are options: Got no time? Bake a loaf of banana-poi bread on the weekend, slice it up, and grab and portion on your way out the door. Got a few minutes? Make an oatmeal cake ahead of time; run it under the broiler in the morning so it's warm and the toppings are bubbly. Got a leisurely morning? Make a heaping pan of Kālua Pork Hash.

Whatever you pick, start the day sunny side up.

Sandy Kodama is known as "Mom," not just to her six children, but also to the staff and many of the customers at Sansei Seafood Restaurant & Sushi Bar.

Her son, D.K., owns the place, and she's his secret weapon.

She greets customers, serves tables, pours water, helps train the kitchen staff, and cooks, too. Most important to the guys in the Star-Bulletin newsroom, she usually bakes oatmeal cake on Fridays. It's a dense, flavorful cake, but what the guys like is the topping—a hearty, heavy mixture of coconut, walnuts, and macadamia nuts.

This recipe's for them.

Update: Sandy Kodama died in 2008, but is still remembered for her graciousness as a hostess. Sansei has moved to the Waikiki Beach Marriott from its location near the newsroom.

SANDY KODAMA'S OATMEAL CAKE
Serves 12

1½ cups boiling water
1 cup oatmeal (not instant)
1 cup white sugar
1 cup brown sugar
2 eggs, well beaten
½ cup butter
1⅓ cups flour
1 teaspoon cinnamon
1 teaspoon baking soda
1 teaspoon salt

Topping
6 tablespoons butter
¼ cup evaporated milk
½ cup brown sugar
½ teaspoon vanilla
1 cup shredded coconut
1 cup chopped walnuts
1 cup chopped macadamia nuts (optional)

Heat oven to 350°F. Grease a 9 x 13-inch pan.

Pour water over oatmeal and let stand 20 minutes. Add sugars, eggs, and butter. Mix until well combined.

Combine flour, cinnamon, baking soda, and salt. Stir into oatmeal mixture. Pour into prepared pan. Bake 30 minutes.

Combine topping ingredients and spread over baked cake. Place under broiler until bubbly and golden.

The bread pudding at Agnes' Portuguese Bake Shop in Kailua is a rich blend of sweetbread, apples, raisins, and spices.

Chief baker Non DeMello says a fat analysis would be "scary." He offers ways to trim the fat: Try using egg whites only, fat-free evaporated milk, coconut flavoring instead of shredded coconut, and eliminate the butter.

But Non warns that it won't taste the same. His bread pudding is simply not for the calorie-squeamish. It's like buying a Jaguar, he says: "If you have to ask the price, you can't afford it." And if you have to ask for the fat content of his bread pudding, you can't afford the calories.

AGNES' PORTUGUESE BAKE SHOP
BREAD PUDDING
Serves 12

1 (1-pound) Portuguese sweetbread loaf, in ½-inch cubes
1½ cups raisins
⅓ cup flaked coconut, preferably unsweetened
¾ cup peeled, cored and
  chopped apple
¼ cup butter or margarine,
  melted
2 cups evaporated milk
2 cups water
2 cups sugar
4 eggs
2 tablespoons cinnamon
2 teaspoons ground ginger
1 teaspoon nutmeg
½ teaspoon salt
1 cup brown sugar, lightly packed

Heat oven to 350°F to 375°F.

Combine bread, raisins, coconut, and apple. Drizzle butter over mixture and lightly toss.

In a separate bowl, whisk together the evaporated milk, water, sugar, eggs, cinnamon, ginger, nutmeg, and salt, making sure the sugar is completely dissolved.

Pour liquid mixture into the bread mixture. Stir to combine, but do not over mix (don't let bread cubes get too soggy).

Allow mix to sit about 15 minutes. Pour into a greased 9 x 13-inch pan. Spread brown sugar evenly over the top.

Place pan into a larger pan filled with water. Bake 50 minutes to 1 hour, until the pudding has "puffed" a little and springs back to the touch. Cool before cutting. Refrigerate leftovers.

Everyone's got a favorite banana bread recipe, so for one to stand out, it's got to have a something extra. In this recipe, from Lisa Siu of Kaka'ako Kitchen, it's poi. Her loaf contains ¼ cup of poi, but if you fear the pasty gray stuff, don't worry: this bread will not turn out all health-foody and strange. It also includes butter, sugar, eggs, and sour cream.

Taro, the sole ingredient (save water) in poi, has a few advantages in baking. Taro is high in a substance called soluble gum, which provides a "mouthfeel" of thickness and richness, even though taro is fat-free. This property of taro is unique among starches. Potatoes don't have it. Oatmeal is close, but its high fiber content produces a grainier baked good, whereas poi gives you a smooth, soft bread (imagine taro rolls). This all gives the Kaka'ako poi bread its advantage.

KAKA'AKO KITCHEN
BANANA-POI BREAD
Makes 1 loaf

½ cup butter
1¼ cup sugar
¼ cup poi
2 teaspoons vanilla
2 eggs
¼ cup sour cream
1 cup mashed overripe bananas
1½ cups flour (all-purpose or bread flour)
1 teaspoon baking soda
½ teaspoon salt

Heat oven to 350°F.

Cream butter, sugar, poi, and vanilla until fluffy. Add eggs one at a time, then mix in sour cream and bananas.

Combine flour, baking soda, and salt. Add to wet ingredients and stir to combine. Do not over mix. Pour batter into an ungreased 9 x 5-inch loaf pan. Bake 45 to 55 minutes.

Oatmeal cakes have been on the menu at Big City Diner since the restaurant opened. The ingredients—oatmeal, sugar, water, and raisins—are cooked up just like your regular Quaker Oats, but it's a much thicker mix. So thick that when patted into a pan, it firms up into a "cake" dense enough to slice. Wedges are then browned on the griddle.

You'll notice that the cakes are almost fat-free, but they do include a lot of brown sugar. If you prefer, you could easily cut back on the sugar or use a sugar substitute.

BIG CITY DINER OATMEAL CAKES

Serves 6

8 cups water
1½ teaspoons salt
2 tablespoons cinnamon
1 cup brown sugar, packed
½ heaping cup raisins
6 cups quick-cooking oatmeal
1 tablespoon butter

Combine water, salt, cinnamon, and sugar in large pot. Bring to boil.

Add raisins and oatmeal. Cook over medium heat, stirring frequently, until very thick, 3 to 5 minutes. Spread evenly in a 13 x 9-inch pan and let cool.

Cut into 6 squares, then cut each square in half diagonally to form 12 wedges.

Melt butter in skillet and brown each wedge lightly on all sides, including cut edges (to keep oatcake nearly fat free, use a cooking oil spray instead of butter). Serve with honey and fresh fruit.

Bread pudding is a classic way to use up leftovers. Of course, keeping the bread from going to waste requires an additional investment in eggs and cream, but then you get to eat a nice, warm slice of bread pudding. Probably worth it.

At O'ahu Country Club the bread pudding is made from dinner rolls, sliced to give it a nice appearance and texture.

To pull it off I suggest using a disposable foil pan, 10 x 12 inches and 2½ to 3 inches deep, easy to find in supermarkets. Get a larger pan, too, as you're going to need to set up a water bath, which means the smaller pan has to fit inside the larger one, with room to spare.

Oh, and here's a tip: It will be easier to slice the bread if it's frozen.

O'AHU COUNTRY CLUB
BREAD PUDDING
Serves 12

1¼ pounds dinner rolls (preferred) or day-old white bread
¼ cup raisins, optional
9 large eggs
2¼ cups sugar
¼ teaspoon salt
¾ tablespoon vanilla extract
7 cups whole milk
2 cups heavy cream

Heat oven to 350°F. Spray a 10 x 12-inch pan with cooking oil spray.

Slice dinner rolls or break bread into pieces. Place in pan. Sprinkle with raisins, if using, and set aside.

Beat eggs and add sugar, salt, and vanilla; whisk until fluffy. Add milk and cream; mix well, then strain (this mixture is called guss). Pour evenly over bread in pan. Make sure bread absorbs most of the guss.

Spray sheet of foil with cooking oil spray. Cover pan loosely with foil. Place pan into larger pan to create water bath. Place pans in oven. Add warm water to outer pan, about halfway up the sides. Bake 90 minutes.

Check pudding for doneness. Top should be firm, but center might be a little jiggly. It will set as it cools. Serve warm.

Paul Chun, president and chief executive officer of Chun Kim Chow Ltd., died June 21 at age eighty-four. His company had extensive real estate and retail holdings, including the Robins shoe stores and the Waikiki Circle Hotel. But his hobby was cooking. "Every Sunday was an extravagant nine-course meal," his daughter, Pamela Chun-Ganske, says.

During the West Coast dock strike in 1971, the hotel ran out of pancake mix, so Chun developed a scratch pancake recipe by studying cookbooks in bookstores (he didn't actually buy one, his daughter says).

The recipe became the hotel restaurant's signature; people would line up for the 99¢ plate of two pancakes, eggs, and breakfast meat. At his funeral, the family passed out the recipe. A nice way to remember someone, isn't it?

I gave the recipe a test run, and at first thought something was wrong: there was so much baking powder that the batter got all frothy. But this turns out to be the secret to a light, fluffy pancake.

PAUL CHUN'S PANCAKES

Makes about 12 pancakes

2 cups flour
3 tablespoons baking powder
Dash of salt
3 or 4 tablespoons sugar
3 eggs, separated
1¼ cup milk
⅓ block melted butter, cooled

Combine dry ingredients. Beat yolks slightly and add to dry ingredients, along with a little milk. Stir.

Beat egg whites and add, along with a little more milk. Add melted butter. Stir and gradually add enough of the remaining milk so batter is of the right consistency (this is a judgment call—it shouldn't be too thin and should still have lumps, but needs to be loose enough to scoop easily). Batter will get very fluffy as baking powder activates; do not be alarmed. Do not over mix. Let sit 10 to 15 minutes to settle.

Heat griddle or skillet over medium. Pour about ¼ cup batter for each pancake. Turn when edges are dry and bottom is golden.

Jean Sumimoto was three months old when her father, George Abe, opened a bakery in the back of the Piggly Wiggly store on Oneawa Street in Kailua. The proud papa named the bakery for his baby, calling it Jean's Bakery & Fountain.

This was in 1950. The bakery remained open until 1972, although Abe eventually moved it to a freestanding location on Ulunui Street.

The one recipe that survives from the old bakery is his Danish Tea Cake, a buttermilk cake topped with a maple-flavored glaze and chopped nuts.

Note that Sumimoto and her dad measured out their ingredients by weight, which is the best way to get exact results. For those without scales, though, volume measurements are included here.

JEAN'S BAKERY DANISH TEA CAKE

12 ounces (1¾ cups, unpacked) brown sugar
6 ounces (¾ cup) white sugar
1¼ teaspoon salt
1 teaspoon vanilla
6 ounces (¾ cup) vegetable oil
12 ounces (1½ cups) buttermilk, divided use
11 ounces (2¾ cups) cake flour
1 tablespoon baking powder
1½ teaspoons baking soda
3 large eggs
½ cup chopped macadamia nuts

Glaze
⅔ cup powdered sugar
1 tablespoon water
2 to 3 teaspoons maple syrup

Heat oven to 350°F. Grease and flour two 8-inch round cake pans. Combine sugars, salt, and vanilla. Mix in oil and ½ the buttermilk.

Sift together flour, baking powder, and baking soda. Add to sugar mixture. Add remaining buttermilk and eggs. Mix well (batter will be very thin). Pour into prepared pans. Bake about 40 minutes. Let cool.

To make glaze: Combine ingredients and stir until smooth. Drizzle cake with glaze and sprinkle with chopped nuts.

Vicky Cayetano, the former first lady, enjoys baking, but doesn't have a lot for time for it. "In fact, I've never seen my wife bake anything," former Governor Ben says.

Mrs. Cayetano, though, says the art runs in her family, her father being big on baking and her mother having a sweet tooth. The result: cakes every week, birthdays or not.

This brings us to her family recipe for an apple cake: The cake is more appley than cakey—Mrs. Cayetano says her father was committed to healthy cooking. It's also fairly flat, like a bar cookie, but soft like a cake. There's plenty of apple flavor, spiced with cinnamon and nutmeg. "It's not real attractive," she says, "but it tastes good."

FIRST LADY'S
FRESH APPLE SPICE CAKE

4 cups diced apples
1¹/₃ cup sugar
2 cups sifted flour
2 teaspoons cinnamon
½ teaspoon nutmeg
½ teaspoon salt
2 teaspoons baking soda
²/₃ cup chopped walnuts
²/₃ cup golden raisins
2 eggs
½ cup canola oil
2 teaspoons vanilla extract

Heat oven to 350°F. Butter a 9 x 13-inch baking pan.

Combine apples, sugar, flour, cinnamon, nutmeg, salt, baking soda, walnuts, and raisins. Toss to mix well. Set aside.

Combine eggs, oil, and vanilla. Blend until smooth. Add to apple mixture and stir until well-blended. Spread evenly in baking pan. Bake 45 to 60 minutes until a pick inserted in center comes out clean. Cool.

This dish comes from the benefit brunch that Leeward Community College throws every year to raise funds for culinary scholarships. It is credited to chef-instructor Ian Riseley, who thoughtfully broke it down from a serving size of 300.

Except for boiling the potatoes it's a pretty quick project, with results that belie its simplicity.

KĀLUA PIG AND GREEN ONION HASH
Serves 8

1 pound russet potatoes, peeled and quartered
1 medium onion, finely chopped
1 ounce (2 tablespoons) butter
1 pound kālua pork, cooked, roughly chopped
4 egg yolks
½ cup chopped green onion (green part only)
Salt and pepper, to taste
1 cup panko (Japanese breadcrumbs)
1 cup vegetable oil

Cook potatoes in boiling salted water until soft, about 20 minutes. Drain and let dry 10 minutes, then lightly mash. A few small lumps are all right.

Meanwhile, sauté onion in butter until soft and light brown, about 5 minutes.

Mix mashed potatoes with cooked onion, kālua pork, egg yolks, and green onions. Taste and season with salt and pepper. Form mixture into 8 patties. Press panko onto both sides of each patty.

Heat oil in skillet to 350°F. Fry patties until golden brown on both sides, working in batches. Drain on paper towels.

I f you like soft-boiled eggs (like me) and fried food (like me), this little puff ball will make you so very happy.

Colin Hazama, executive chef at the Royal Hawaiian, prepared this tidbit as part of a larger plate for a cooking competition. It was magical—a soft-cooked egg, stripped of its shell, rolled in panko and deep-fried. It emerged crispy on the outside, soft with a runny yolk on the inside.

Hazama said he perfected the technique while working with chef Jean-Georges Vongerichten, who served the crispy eggs with caviar at his acclaimed restaurant, Jean-Georges in New York. "It's very ingenious," Hazama says.

It's also a little tricky and you'll have to try very hard and be very patient and maybe waste a few eggs. I did.

I've dumbed down the process a little, because obviously there's a difference between us and the professionals: Hazama's crew made 320 eggs for the competition. I had my hands full making two. But I'll get better at it.

CRISPY SOFT-BOILED EGGS

Serves 4

4 eggs
Bowl of ice water
½ cup fine panko (see note)
Vegetable oil, for frying

Fill a saucepan with ½ inch of water; bring to boil. Gently lower eggs into water; cover and lower heat to medium. Cook 6 minutes then immediately place eggs in ice water.

Gently break shells, then peel each egg. A small spoon can be used to separate egg from shell if it's stubborn. If you break the yolk that egg is a lost cause.

Cover eggs in panko and let sit while oil is heating. The panko should make a light coating, but if it doesn't stick, wet the eggs with water, milk, or an egg wash first.

Heat oil to 330°F in a small pot. Carefully lower 1 egg into oil and fry a few seconds until golden all around. Remove from oil and drain on paper towels, then fry remaining eggs.

Note: Fine panko can be purchased, or pulverize regular panko in a blender.

Variations: Once you master the basics here, you can try jazzing up the coating. Hazama adds ground macadamia-nut cookies and Diamond Bakery soda crackers to his. I've seen versions with Parmesan cheese and pulverized bacon. You can get as wild as you like.

When we were vacationing in Tokyo, we attempted to save time and money by eating breakfast in our hotel room, mostly quick bites we picked up at convenience stores the night before (the food in Tokyo 7-Elevens would amaze you).

For me it was almost always tamagoyaki — a rolled egg omelet (literally "egg grilled"). In the U.S. tamagoyaki mostly shows up as a thin slice atop nigiri sushi, but in Tokyo shops it is sold in slabs with various flavorings. You slice it yourself to reveal the delicate layers rolled inside.

A single-serve takeout version made a high-protein breakfast for about a dollar.

I became obsessed with making this at home, which seemed a possibility after watching a few YouTube videos, even though tamagoyaki is tricky. You have to roll up the omelet as it cooks, then add more layers of egg and roll several more times. Japanese chefs accomplish this with chopsticks and skillful tossing of the pan. Beginners might need two wide spatulas (I have graduated to two small spatulas).

For authenticity this dish requires a special square or rectangular pan with a nonstick surface and straight sides about 1½ inches high (stocked locally at Don Quijote and Marukai stores). It can be made in a regular round skillet, but you won't get the nice straight sides.

Tamagoyaki is often made with sugar and turns out quite sweet. I have opted for a more savory version that instead uses mirin and furikake for a slight salty edge.

NOT-TOO-SWEET
TAMAGOYAKI WITH FURIKAKE
Serves 2 as side dish

4 large eggs (or 3 jumbo eggs)
¼ cup chicken broth
3 tablespoons mirin (Japanese sweet cooking wine)
2 tablespoons vegetable oil
2 tablespoons furikake (dried seaweed flakes)

Beat eggs with broth and mirin.

Place a square or rectangular tamagoyaki pan over medium-low heat and coat generously with oil. Pour a thin layer of egg mixture into pan. Egg should sizzle and bubble a little, but if it seems to be cooking too fast, lift the pan off the heat. Break any bubbles. Lift egg to let runny parts fill in underneath. Sprinkle with furikake.

When egg is nearly set but still wet, use a spatula to loosen edges. Carefully lift omelet on one side and fold over a strip about 2 inches wide. Continue folding over the omelet to make a roll at the other end of the pan.

Coat pan with more oil, including beneath the cooked portion. Pour another layer of egg into pan, letting some run under first roll. Sprinkle with furikake. Fold over first roll and keep rolling to incorporate new layer of egg.

Repeat once or twice to use up egg mixture.

Turn omelet onto plate and cut into slices or cubes.

I am a Tolkien geek, without apology. I have read *The Hobbit* and the *Lord of the Rings* trilogy too many times to count, including all the appendices ("Annals of Kings and Rulers," fascinating!). I can tell you how the wizards Gandalf, Saruman, and Radagast got to Middle-earth; how Middle-earth was formed. I can tell you … oh, never mind.

When *The Hobbit: An Unexpected Journey* (the movie) opened I had an itch to somehow find a tie-in with food. Luckily, in *The Hobbit* (the book) there is much food, hobbits being hungry creatures who try to eat at least six meals a day. I can tell you what those meals are … oh, never mind.

Near the beginning of the book, thirteen ravenous dwarfs sit down for a meal and the dwarf Balin calls out: "I wouldn't mind some cake — seed cake, if you have any."

A seed cake is similar to a coffee cake in that it is dense, not too sweet, and could be served with butter or jam. The usual flavorings are nutmeg and caraway, the seed that gives rye bread its distinctive taste. Applied lightly, caraway gives the cake a mild, mysterious flavor.

Hobbits eat it and so do real people, mostly in England, with their tea.

I snuck mine into the movie theater and ate it just as the dwarfs were sitting down to eat.

HOBBIT SEED CAKE
Makes 1 (9-inch) cake

2½ cups flour
1 teaspoon baking powder
½ teaspoon nutmeg
¾ cup butter, softened
¾ cup sugar
3 large eggs
1 cup milk
2 teaspoons caraway seeds
2 tablespoons brown sugar

Heat oven to 350°F. Grease a 9-inch round cake pan. Line bottom with a circle of baking parchment.

Sift together flour, baking powder, and nutmeg.

In another bowl, cream butter and sugar on medium speed of electric mixer until fluffy. Beat in eggs one at a time until well combined. Gradually beat in flour mixture. Blend in milk a little at a time. Batter will be thick but will pour out of the bowl. Add a little more milk if necessary.

Fold in caraway seeds. Pour batter into baking pan. Sprinkle brown sugar evenly over top. Bake 40 to 50 minutes, until a pick inserted into the center comes out clean.

herb's scout stew

yen king spareribs

MEAT LOVERS

This is the protein chapter, all about the center of the plate. Some vegetables have crept into the soups and stews, but for the most part the recipes are big and beefy or plump and porky.

Protein is back in style, by the way, so there's no reason to feel guilty if you just can't make a meal without a meaty main dish. Balance is the key. Have a salad on the side.

Carnivores, enter here.

When people tell you you've got the best spareribs on the island, you don't argue about it, even if you can't really explain why.

Tony Choi, owner of Big-Way Burger in Wahiawā, says people tell him they come from far and wide just for his spareribs. "The Kahala post office will send someone out once in awhile."

It's a very basic recipe: Sugar, vinegar, shoyu, and ginger. What's the secret? "I don't know," Tony says. "Maybe it's the browning on the grill."

Update: Bigway Burger closed in 2003.

BIG-WAY BURGER
SWEET-AND-SOUR SPARERIBS
Serves 20

10 pounds spareribs, cut in 2-inch cubes
1²/₃ cups sugar
3 cups vinegar
3 cups soy sauce
¾ cup crushed ginger
1½ tablespoons cornstarch

Brown meat, then transfer to a pot.

Add water to cover the meat halfway. Bring to a boil, then lower heat and cook 1 hour.

Add remaining ingredients, except cornstarch, and simmer 20 to 30 minutes. Meat should be tender but not soft enough to fall off the bone.

Mix cornstarch with water until smooth and add to ribs to thicken sauce.

Serve on a bed of cabbage with two scoops rice and kim chee.

Howard Co opened Yen King in Kahala Mall eighteen years ago, after a successful stint as co-owner and manager of King Tsin restaurant, where he learned to cook.

Co boils his cooking strategy down to a mantra—high heat, short time. He says all you need to succeed is a knowledge of how long various foods take to cook, so you know in what order to throw them into the pot.

These spareribs are a Peking-style dish.

Update: Yen King has closed at Kahala Mall, but many of the cooks moved on to Maple Garden on Isenberg Street, when it was taken over by long-time Yen King employee Richard Lam.

YEN KING SPARERIBS IN ORANGE PEEL AND HONEY SAUCE

Serves 4

1 pound spareribs, in 1-inch cubes, washed and drained
2-inch piece ginger, peeled
2 stalks green onion
1 tablespoon white wine
3 quarts water
Oil for frying and finishing
Dash of soy sauce

Honey Syrup

1 teaspoon vegetable oil
2 tablespoons chicken broth
2 tablespoons honey
1 teaspoon minced orange peel
1 tablespoon soy sauce

Place spareribs, ginger, green onion, wine and water in a pot and bring to a boil. Lower heat, cover and cook 2 hours. Drain.

Heat oil to 400°F and deep-fry spareribs 3 minutes. Drain.

To prepare syrup: Heat wok for 10 seconds, then add all ingredients. Add fried spareribs and stir vigorously for 1 minute until coated in a thick syrup. Quickly add a dash more oil and soy sauce. Toss mixture a few times.

The Paniolo Beef Stew served at the Hale Koa Hotel is Hawaiian in name, but not in flavor. Think of it as paniolo equals cowboy equals southwestern.

Rolf Walter, the hotel's executive chef, said the dish is basically a beef stew with peppers, in a Tex-Mex style.

I've adapted the recipe from an original that serves fifty. It makes a flavorful pot of stew that owes a great deal of its distinctive taste to Dijon mustard.

HALE KOA PANIOLO BEEF STEW
Serves 12

¼ cup vegetable oil
5 pounds stew meat, cubed
½ cup flour
1 large onion, sliced thin
3 large tomatoes, seeded, in ½-inch dice
2 ounces serrano chilies, seeded and diced (use gloves when handling)
3 large cloves garlic, minced
¼ cup packed brown sugar
1 (12-ounce) can beer
2 cups water
¾ cup Dijon mustard
½ teaspoon ground cumin
1 teaspoon oregano
¾ teaspoon allspice
½ teaspoon cayenne pepper
½ teaspoon salt, or to taste
1 green bell pepper, julienned
1 red bell pepper julienned

1 cup frozen corn kernels, defrosted and drained
Cilantro leaves, for garnish

Heat 1 tablespoon of the oil in a large skillet. Pat beef cubes dry and dredge in flour, shaking off excess. Brown meat on all sides, working in batches; add more oil with each batch. Place in a large pot.

Sauté onions in the same skillet until soft. Add tomatoes, chilies, garlic and brown sugar. Add beer and deglaze—scraping bottom of pan to loosen any browned bits. Add mixture to meat in pot.

Add water, mustard, and spices to pot and bring to a boil, stirring often. Reduce heat and simmer about 1½ hours, until meat is tender. Skim fat.

Add bell peppers and corn; cook 5 more minutes. Garnish with cilantro.

Note: The recipe calls for seeding the serrano chilies, which tames a lot of the heat. The Hale Koa original called for a lot more than I used, but I'll leave the exact amount up to you. My supermarket serranos were still pretty frisky after seeding, so adjust the amount based on the freshness of your peppers and your own tolerance, not to mention how much time you want to devote to the laborious task of seeding (be sure to use gloves when handling the peppers).

September 12, 2001

Wilson Wu, chef and co-owner of On On Kapahulu, says these pork chops and another Chinese favorite, salt-and-pepper shrimp, are made exactly the same way. He cooks, by the way, by eyeball, with no written measurements, so this recipe is based on his approximations and my observation of the technique.

It's a simple recipe, though, so taste and make adjustments. After a few tries you should have it right.

ON ON SALT-PEPPER PORK CHOPS
Serves 2

1 pound thin-sliced pork chops, cut in thirds with bone left on
Vegetable oil for frying
1 teaspoon flour
1 tablespoon minced garlic
2 large red chili peppers, sliced (about 2 tablespoons)
¼ teaspoon salt, or more to taste
½ teaspoon cooking wine
2 tablespoons chopped green onions

Fill wok with enough oil to just cover meat and heat to 350°F over medium.

Toss pork with flour. Drop into hot oil and toss a couple of times. Quickly add garlic, peppers, and salt, then wine, stirring the entire time. Add green onions, toss once, then strain oil.

Many people swear by the mango chutney, but for legions of others it's the Portuguese Bean Soup that marks the Punahou Carnival with good taste.

Thankfully, the school is willing to share.

The soup is especially filling, with cabbage and macaroni cooked in.

To cut the fat in this soup, try a technique recommended in other similar recipes: Cook the ham hocks a day ahead and refrigerate the broth. The next day, remove the hardened layer of fat atop the broth, then complete the soup.

PUNAHOU PORTUGUESE
BEAN SOUP
Makes 10 large servings

1 pound ham hocks
2 (14-ounce) cans kidney beans
2 large potatoes, cubed
3 large carrots, diced
1 medium onion, chopped
1 cup chopped celery
1 (16-ounce) can crushed tomatoes
1 (16-ounce) can tomato sauce
1 pound Portuguese sausage, diced or cubed
1 cup uncooked macaroni
1 teaspoon granulated garlic
1 tablespoon sugar
Salt and pepper to taste
1 medium head of cabbage, cubed

Boil ham hocks in 2 quarts water until tender (save stock). Cut meat from the bones.

Bring ham stock to a boil and add the cut meat and all the remaining ingredients except the cabbage. Simmer for 1 hour, stirring frequently. If too thick, add a little water. Add the cabbage, cook until tender.

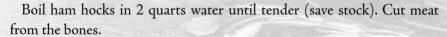

Given all the stresses of hanging out at a hospital, a dish spooned up in the cafeteria is not what you'd normally think of as comfort food. But the beef stew served at the Queen's Hospital cafeteria does seem to work for hospital visitors.

Vivian Coppock, director of food services at Queen's Medical Center, said the stew is on the menu daily and is very popular.

She provides an interesting perspective on stew, which we tend to think of as a universal dish. The Queen's version, she says, is very different from what she's seen served on the mainland. The beef is cut smaller here, for one thing, and potatoes don't play as big a role (got rice, that's why).

That said, here's the recipe. Nothing fancy, but if it can provide solace to people visiting hospitalized friends and relatives, it must be comfort food indeed.

QUEEN'S HOSPITAL BEEF STEW
Serves 8

1 teaspoon vegetable oil
2 pounds beef, cut in 1-inch square pieces
1½ cups diced onion
1 teaspoon salt
1 teaspoon pepper
2 beef bouillon cubes
1½ cups water
2 bay leaves
½ cup tomato paste
½ cup canned, diced tomatoes
1 teaspoon chili pepper sauce, such as Tobasco
2 cups diced celery
1½ cups diced carrot
2⅛ cups diced potato
2 tablespoons cornstarch, dissolved in ¼ cup cold water
¼ cup frozen peas

Heat oil in skillet. Brown meat over medium heat. Add onions and cook until onions are transparent. Add salt, pepper, beef bouillon cubes, water, bay leaves, tomato paste, diced tomatoes, and pepper sauce.

Bring to a boil, then reduce heat to low and simmer until meat is tender. Add more water if necessary.

Add celery, carrots, and potatoes; simmer until vegetables are tender.

Add cornstarch mixture to stew. Simmer a few minutes. Add peas and simmer 4 minutes.

Every Memorial Day, Dr. Jack Scaff, trainer of marathoners, opens his Round Top Drive Home to serious chili cooks, all competing for the championship in the Great Hawaiian Chili Cookoff. The winner of the top prize goes on to the International Chili Society's World Cookoff in Las Vegas.

The contestants are all serious pursuers of the art of chili, which means they don't use ground beef and they barely use beans. Their chili is chunky with beef, pork, and sausage, slow-cooked with onions, peppers, and specialized combinations of spices.

The 1999 winner was Jerry Hall of 'Ewa Beach, who called his concoction Jerry's Junkyard Chili. His recipe made 2 gallons.

It is my favorite chili recipe, although I've adapted it to make a smaller batch and I do add beans. The instructions aren't especially difficult to follow, but it takes a lot of time to prep all the meat.

JUNKYARD CHILI
Makes 12 large servings

2 tablespoons vegetable oil
1½ pounds boneless cross-rib roast, in ½- to ¼-inch pieces
1 pound boneless pork, in ½- to ¼-inch pieces
2 medium onions, diced
1 tablespoon crushed garlic
1 (15-ounce) can chicken broth
½ cup chili powder (Gebhardt brand preferred)
¼ cup cumin
2 (15-ounce) cans tomato sauce
1 large green bell pepper, diced
1 large red bell pepper, diced
½ pound Portuguese sausage, sliced
1 jalapeño pepper, minced
2 (14.5-ounce) cans kidney beans

Heat oil in large pot. Brown meat, onions, and garlic. Stir in broth; cover and simmer 30 minutes.

Add remaining ingredients except beans and simmer 2 hours.

Stir in beans. Simmer until heated through.

Mustard cabbage—sin choy in Chinese—is a dark, slightly bitter green that's delicious when pickled.

This stir-fry dish is a sweet-sour mixture that's balanced just right to put all the best flavors forward. It's easy and quick. I'll often slice everything up and prepare the marinade in the morning so that I can stir up the dish quickly after work.

Use less beef and more veggies if you like: crisp vegetables such as sliced celery, bell peppers, and carrots work better than softer vegetables like zucchini or eggplant.

Pickled sin choy is sold in packages in Asian markets and Chinatown groceries.

BEEF WITH PICKLED
MUSTARD CABBAGE
Serves 4

1 pound lean sliced beef
2 tablespoons vegetable oil
1-inch piece ginger, smashed and minced
1 small onion, sliced
2 cups (one 10-ounce package) sliced pickled mustard cabbage (sin choy)
2 tablespoons cornstarch dissolved in 2 tablespoons water

Marinade
2 tablespoons sugar
2 tablespoons soy sauce
2 tablespoons oyster sauce
2 tablespoons red wine or whisky
1 teaspoon sesame oil

Combine marinade ingredients and mix with beef. Let sit 30 minutes at room temperature.

Heat oil in skillet. Add ginger and stir-fry until fragrant. Remove beef from marinade, reserving ¼ cup marinade, and add beef to skillet. Add onions and stir-fry until beef is partly cooked. Add mustard cabbage with liquid from package, plus reserved marinade. Sitr-fry until beef is cooked. Thicken with cornstarch mixture.

Herb Yasukochi, longtime Scout master for the Honpa Hongwanji Hawai'i Betsuin, is accustomed to taking fifty or sixty boys on week-long summer camps, during which bulk cooking is the order of the day.

But for the annual Taste of Hongwanji bazaar, Yasukochi makes beef stew using a proven recipe filled with beef chuck, short ribs, and Portuguese sausage.

Yasukochi, a service manager for The Gas Co., has been involved with the Scouts since childhood, serving as a leader since his sons joined the temple troop twenty-one years ago.

He also leads cooking classes for Scouts. Boys are enthusiastic about cooking, he says, if it means they get to eat well. The results are surprising to parents. "They'll say, 'Mr. Y, you know what happened? You taught my boy to cook, so we had stir-fry all weekend.'"

HERB'S SCOUT STEW
Serves 20

¼ cup vegetable oil, divided
2 pounds beef chuck roast, cubed
1 pound boneless beef short ribs, in bite-sized pieces
6 cloves garlic, smashed
2 teaspoons chicken base (see note)
2 teaspoons beef base (see note)
2 (15-ounce) cans tomato sauce
1 (6-ounce) can tomato paste
1 (3-inch) piece ginger, peeled and sliced
4 bay leaves
1 pound carrots, sliced
6 medium potatoes, cubed
6 onions, chopped
6 stalks celery, sliced
1 tablespoon Hawaiian salt
12 ounces Portuguese sausage, sliced
1 (11-ounce) can corn
½ cup soy sauce
2 tablespoons flour
¼ cup water

Heat half of the oil in a stock pot; brown beef, ribs, and garlic. Add chicken and beef base, tomato sauce, tomato paste, ginger, and bay leaves to pot. Add water to cover ingredients. Simmer 1 hour over medium-high heat until meat is tender.

Brown carrots, potatoes, onions, and celery in remaining oil in a wok or skillet. Season with Hawaiian salt. Add vegetables, sausage, and corn to stock pot and simmer another 30 minutes.

Combine soy sauce, flour, and water; stir until smooth. Add to pot to thicken. Taste and adjust seasonings with more salt if necessary.

Note: Chicken and beef base are paste-like soup concentrates. They are sold in supermarkets near the bouillons and stocks.

The Golden Dragon roared its last on February 3. After fifty years, the Hilton Hawaiian Village's Chinese restaurant fell victim to a decline in business. Another longtime local restaurant gone, but not forgotten.

It was the Mongolian Lamb that one reader missed most—"one of the best meat dishes I've ever eaten," she said.

The dish, from Golden Dragon chef Steve Chiang, centers on strips of lamb loin marinated in a mixture rich with brandy. The lamb is quickly stir-fried, then given another dose of brandy—along with hoisin, soy sauce, and sugar—in a sauce.

GOLDEN DRAGON
MONGOLIAN LAMB
Serves 2

6 ounces lamb loin, sliced
3 tablespoons vegetable oil
½ piece ginger, in strips
4 stalks green onion, in 2-inch pieces

Marinade
1 tablespoon cornstarch
1 tablespoon oil
1 tablespoon water
1 tablespoon brandy

Sauce
2 tablespoons soy sauce
1 tablespoon hoisin sauce
1 tablespoon brandy
1 tablespoon sugar
1 tablespoon sesame oil
¼ cup chicken stock
1 tablespoon cornstarch

Combine marinade ingredients and marinate lamb 2 hours.

To make sauce: Bring all ingredients to a boil, thickening with cornstarch. Set aside.

Heat wok and add vegetable oil. Add lamb and stir-fry until done. Add ginger and green onion, then add sauce.

*A*t the old Crouching Lion, the dish they called Slavonic Steak was finished tableside in sauté pans filled with butter and garlic. No wonder it made such an impression.

Robert Denis, now chef at Don Ho's Island Grill, is a longtime employee of the restaurants owned by Fred Livingston. These included the Crouching Lion.

He gave me his analysis of its appeal: "It's like an M&M: it just melts in the mouth." Plus, "any time you use butter you can't fail."

Update: Do Ho's Island Grill closed in 2011.

CROUCHING LION SLAVONIC STEAK
Serves 4

2 (8-ounce) pieces filet mignon or
   New York strip steak
2 tablespoons butter
½ teaspoon minced garlic
Chopped parsley, for garnish

Marinade
1 cup olive oil
1 tablespoon minced garlic
⅛ cup chopped fresh herbs (thyme, rosemary and parsley)
1 tablespoon cracked black pepper

Whisk together marinade ingredients. Place filet mignon in marinade; refrigerate overnight.

The next day, heat sauté pan with a hint of olive oil. Remove steak from marinade and pan-sear until rare.

Gently heat a separate sauté pan. Add butter and garlic, cooking until garlic is lightly brown.

Slice steak and place in pan with butter. Cook to desired doneness. Sprinkle with parsley.

Chef Mariano Lalica of the Oceanarium Restaurant at the Pacific Beach Hotel needed a new dish for the carving station at his Sunday brunch buffet. He considered the matter and came up with … pork belly. Not Chinese, not Filipino, but Korean.

Lalica's pork belly glazed with a kalbi-style sauce is actually a mash-up of Korean, Thai, and Chinese flavors, with Japanese mirin thrown in for good measure.

The dish takes two days—one for a long braise in a flavorful broth, the second for roasting.

In between, the meat and the cooking broth chill in the refrigerator in separate containers. This separation is important. The meat dries slightly and forms a crust, Lalica said, and the broth separates so that you can skim off the fat.

The process "relaxes the meat, and when you reheat it, it becomes nice and tender."

I gave the recipe a spin, and despite all the grating and chopping, it was not hard. And it was great. Seriously great. The braise-rest-roast process turns that lovely layer of pork belly fat into a chewy yet tender band of deliciousness that was not at all greasy.

Serve it chopped over rice or sliced in bao buns, with extra sauce on the side. Deliver it to a potluck and you will be a hero.

Update: The Oceanarium closed in late 2016. The Pacific Beach Hotel is undergoing renovation. Celebrity chef Masaharu Morimoto will have two restaurants in the revamped resort, to be called 'Alohilani.

OCEANARIUM
KALBI-GLAZED PORK BELLY
Serves 12

5 pounds pork belly
1 cup sugar
1 cup soy sauce
1 cup Thai sweet chili sauce
4 cups water
1 cup mirin (Japanese sweet rice cooking wine)
1 small onion, finely grated
1 small Asian pear, peeled and finely grated (or substitute a
   sweet apple)
¼ cup minced garlic
¼ cup minced ginger
2 tablespoons sesame oil
¼ teaspoon black pepper
2 green onions, cut in 1-inch pieces
1 bunch cilantro, chopped

Place pork belly fat side up in a large pot or pan.

Combine remaining ingredients and pour over pork belly. Bring to simmer over medium-high heat, then reduce heat and simmer, covered, 2½ hours, or until pork belly is soft.

Carefully remove meat from liquid and place in single layer in pan. Refrigerate uncovered overnight.

Strain cooking broth into a separate container; cover and refrigerate.

The next day, remove fat from cooking liquid. Pour into saucepan and bring to boil, then reduce heat and simmer until thickened (reducing to a very syrupy sauce will take about an hour).

Heat oven to 325°F. Remove meat from refrigerator and place in roasting pan. Brush with sauce and roast for 30 to 45 minutes, brushing with sauce every 10 minutes, until heated through and dark golden brown.

Let rest a few minutes, then slice. Serve with extra sauce.

waialua chicken wings

butterfish niitsuke

CHICKEN 'N' SEAFOOD

I n the protein universe, you've got your red meats, your poultry, and your seafood. The second two are generally thought of as lighter, but that's really untrue.

Fried chicken or a creamy seafood sauce would give the fat content in a lot of beef dishes a real run for the money.

So what's my point? Balance and variety in all things.

This collection of entrée dishes includes restaurant favorites and home-style classics, in a range of preparations, from the diet-conscious to the diet-buster.

Consider your circumstances and make your picks.

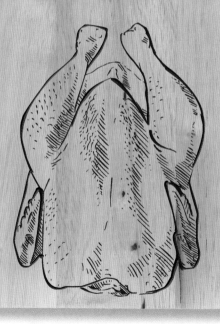

Lots of people consider the katsu at L&L Drive-Inn to be the gold standard in plate-lunch fare.

Eddie Flores, owner of the L&L empire, has been very generous with this recipe, sharing it not only with *Star-Bulletin* readers, but allowing me to pass it on for printing in a couple of benefit cookbooks. No doubt it lent brand-name value that helped sell a few copies for various good causes.

Eddie says chicken katsu is one of the most popular L&L dishes, right up there with barbecue chicken and short ribs.

Update: Flores has expanded the L&L empire through franchisees who've opened restaurants across the mainland. Outside Hawai'i they're called L&L Hawaiian Barbecue.

L&L DRIVE-INN CHICKEN KATSU
Serves 10

15 to 20 chicken thighs, about 4 pounds, boned and skinned
1 pound panko

Batter
2 eggs
¾ cup cornstarch
¼ teaspoon salt
¼ teaspoon white pepper
¼ teaspoon garlic powder
1 cup water

Katsu Sauce
¼ cup Worcestershire sauce
½ cup ketchup
½ cup sugar
1¼ cups water
¼ teaspoon salt
$1/8$ teaspoon chicken bouillon
$1/8$ teaspoon white pepper
$1/8$ teaspoon garlic powder
Tabasco sauce to taste

Open the chicken thighs and flatten.
Heat oil to 325°F.
Combine batter ingredients. Coat chicken in batter, then in panko. Fry in oil until brown and crispy.
To make sauce: Combine all ingredients and bring to a boil. To thicken, add a small amount of cornstarch dissolved in water. Chill and serve.
Cut chicken into strips and serve with sauce.

This comfort dish is a signature of the Assaggio Italian restaurant group. It's a simple pasta dish of chicken, mushrooms, and olives, but complexity is added through such flavor boosters as pepperoncini, roasted bell peppers, and capers.

CHICKEN ASSAGGIO
Serves 2

6 ounces fresh island chicken, boned, in strips ¼-inch wide
1 tablespoon extra virgin olive oil
Salt and pepper to taste
⅛ teaspoon dry basil
2 cloves garlic, chopped
¾ cup pepperoncini, diced
1 cup roasted bell peppers
1 tablespoon capers
¾ cup button mushrooms
18 medium black olives
½ cup dry white wine
2 tablespoons butter
5 ounces fresh linguine, cooked

Heat oven to 350°F.

Sear chicken in olive oil in an oven-proof skillet; add salt, pepper, and basil. Bake 5 minutes, or until chicken is cooked through.

Return pan to stove top and add garlic, pepperoncini, bell pepper, capers, mushroom, olives, and wine. Sauté 1 minute, then add butter. Stir until sauce thickens, then serve on a bed of linguine.

Aloha Aina Cafe is an offshoot of Mala 'Ai 'Opio, an organic farm in Wai'anae that goes by its nickname, MA'O Organic, an internship program for low-income youths. Training goes beyond planting and harvesting, however. Marketing is key to success, so the participants are expected to become proficient in that area as well. Thus, they sell their produce at mini-farmers' markets and volunteer at the cafe.

The menu is homespun and simple: banana pancakes, chili, quesadillas, salads made with the farm's organic greens, a killer pumpkin crunch.

Chisa Dodge, the cafe's cook, shared her recipe for chili, which has come to be the one I make for my kids at home. Hardly more complicated than a package mix, but much better.

ALOHA AINA CAFE TURKEY CHILI
Serves 6 to 8

1 pound ground turkey
1½ to 2 cups chopped yellow onion
1 tablespoon vegetable oil
4 cloves garlic, minced, or 1 teaspoon garlic powder
1 tablespoon fresh chopped oregano
1 tablespoon cumin powder
1 cup canned pinto beans
1 cup canned black beans
1½ cups tomatoes sauce
2 tablespoons chili powder, or to taste

Brown turkey and onion in vegetable oil. Add garlic, oregano, and cumin; sauté. Add beans, tomato sauce, and chili powder. Bring to a boil, then reduce heat and simmer 20 minutes.

Revelations that come upon us in hospital beds normally involve self-improvement and self-awareness. We vow to quit smoking, exercise more, and appreciate life and our families to a greater degree, that sort of thing.

June Tong's revelation was a better cookbook.

Laid up for ten days after gallstone surgery, June worked out in her mind the format for an easy-to-use recipe collection where ingredients and instructions were simplified and carefully grouped to make cooking fairly foolproof.

The result was *Popo's Kitchen*, published to mark the bicentennial of Chinese immigration to Hawai'i. It became a standard text in local kitchens; nearly 40,000 copies were sold.

This dish, Bar-B-Que P-Nut Chicken, is one that June used to demonstrate a lot. "When I was selling my cookbook, that would really draw a crowd."

Update: Despite swearing she would never reprint "Popo's Kitchen," June did just that in 2008, publishing several thousand copies of a second volume. She sold most of them out of her own home.

POPO'S BAR-B-QUE
P-NUT CHICKEN
Makes about 12 sticks

5 pounds chicken boneless thighs, cut in cubes

Marinade
1 cup soy sauce
1 cup sugar
1 tablespoon miso
1 tablespoon peanut butter
6 cloves garlic, minced
6 slices ginger, minced
2 tablespoons mirin
½ cup green onion
½ teaspoon garlic chili paste
1 tablespoon sesame oil
1 teaspoon sesame seeds

Combine marinade ingredients and marinate chicken 1 hour. Barbecue on a grill or stir-fry until cooked through. Serve pieces on sticks.

Kengo Nozawa of Kengo's Restaurant remembers his mother serving him a version of this comfort dish. "When I was small, every day my mother would make this for me; that's all we eat."

Dango, or dumplings, take many forms in Japanese soups, from dough balls made of mochi to meatballs made with shrimp, scallop mousse, or even sardines. They may be served in soups with chicken stock, miso, konbu, or dashi as a base.

Kengo's soup includes chicken and lots of vegetables. The dumplings are made with a mixture of mochiko and flour. "Comes out soft, easy to eat," he said. "That's the secret."

KENGO'S KUMAMOTO DANGO JIRU
Serves 8

²/₃ cup bottled tsuyu (see notes)
¼ cup prepared dashi-no-moto
5 cups water
2 pounds boneless chicken thighs, cut in 1½-inch pieces
1 small kabocha (see notes), peeled, seeds and pulp removed, cut in 1½-inch wedges
5 dried shiitake mushrooms, washed, soaked in water until soft and halved; reserve water for stock
4 gobo tempura or vegetable tempura fishcakes, halved
5 small araimo (about 1 pound), blanched and peeled (see notes)
1 pound Chinese cabbage, cut in 1½-inch pieces
1 bunch watercress (about ¾ pound), cut in 1½-inch pieces, for garnish

Dumplings
½ cup flour
½ cup mochiko (sweet rice flour)
½ cup water (or less)

To make dumplings: Combine flour and mochiko; add water slowly, stopping once a stiff dough forms. Knead thoroughly. Form small balls and flatten to silver dollar-size pieces. Drop in boiling water. Dumplings are done when they rise to the surface, about 5 minutes. Makes about 16. Set aside.

To make soup: Bring tsuyu, dashi, and water to a boil. Add chicken; cover and cook on medium heat 10 minutes. Add kabocha, shiitake, and fishcake; reduce heat and simmer 10 minutes. Add araimo, cabbage, and dumplings; simmer another 8 to 10 minutes. Serve in large donburi bowl and garnish with watercress.

Note: Tsuyu is a concentrate made primarily of soy sauce, sugar, and mirin. It is sold in bottles for making broths and sauce for somen, udon, and other soups and dipping sauces. Araimo, also called satoimo, is Japanese taro, smaller than Chinese taro. Kabocha is a small pumpkin, available at most grocery stores. Find tsuyu and araimo at Asian markets.

"You gotta be lucky," says Seiju Ifuku, who founded Rainbow Drive-in with his wife, Ayako. "You gotta have timing. And guts. Little bit guts."

Opening day was October 2, 1961, when Rainbow Drive-In served its first plate lunch in the modest building on Kapahulu Avenue. And that's the way it's been for nearly four decades, under the Rainbow.

In a day, Rainbow Drive-In sells 900 to 1,200 plate lunches and 300 to 500 sandwiches. The menu hasn't changed much—the last time a new item was added was two years ago, roast pork. "My motto is 'Give plenty, and quick service,'" Ifuku says.

RAINBOW DRIVE-IN
SHOYU CHICKEN
Serves 12

12 pounds chicken thighs
¼ cup cornstarch, dissolved in ¼ cup water

Sauce
2½ cups sugar
3¼ cups soy sauce
¾ to 1 cup vinegar
½ teaspoon salt
½ teaspoon pepper
6 dashes Worcestershire sauce
3 to 4 cloves garlic, crushed
3 to 5 inches ginger, crushed

Wash and drain chicken. Combine sauce ingredients.

Combine chicken and sauce in a pot. Bring to a boil, reduce heat, and simmer until chicken is tender, 20 to 30 minutes. Skim sauce. Gradually add cornstarch mixture to thicken sauce (you might not need all the cornstarch). Bring to a boil again and serve.

The best time to make this dish is right after you've had a nice Chinese dinner, provided you ordered roast duck and provided you were able to collect all the bones off everyone's plates.

The dish is Gai See Mein—sometimes spelled Kai See Mein—a noodle dish made with shredded chicken, bamboo shoots, and mushrooms, although it may be dressed up with other veggies, shredded pork, and/or ham, and/or shrimp.

The goodness is in the gravy, though, and for that, you need duck bones.

My best source in the world of Hawai'i-style Chinese cooking, June Tong, author of the 1989 cookbook *Popo's Kitchen*, remembers the dish being a specialty of Lau Yee Chai and popular at many restaurants a generation ago. This is her recipe, reconstructed from memories of her family's version of the dish.

The key is the gravy with its base of duck bones simmered in chicken broth. This is how she makes all her chow mein dishes. "If the gravy is good," she says, "you know the noodles will be good."

GAI SEE MEIN

Serves 4 to 6

¼ cup vegetable oil
2 pounds Hong Kong chow mein noodles
1½ cups shredded cooked chicken
1 cup slivered ham
Diced green onion and cilantro leaves, for garnish

Vegetables
2 tablespoons vegetable oil
1 small onion, sliced
2 stalks celery, sliced
1 carrot, peeled and sliced
½ pound string beans
1 (8-ounce) can bamboo shoot strips
1 (10-ounce) bag bean sprouts
Pinch salt

Gravy
2 (14-ounce) cans chicken broth
Bones from ½ roast duck
1 cup shiitake mushrooms, soaked in hot water, squeezed dry
    and slivered
Salt, to taste
1 tablespoon oyster sauce
¼ cup cornstarch dissolved in ¼ cup water

To make gravy: Bring broth to boil. Add duck bones, mushrooms, salt, and oyster sauce. Simmer 15 to 20 minutes. Remove bones. Thicken with cornstarch mixture.

To prepare noodles: Heat oil in wok or skillet. Pan-fry noodles until slightly crisp. Remove noodles.

To prepare vegetables: Heat oil in same wok. Stir-fry vegetables until tender-crisp, adding bean sprouts last. Season with pinch of salt.

Combine noodles, vegetables, chicken, and ham. Pour hot broth over all. Garnish with green onions and cilantro.

The world gives us many great food combinations: peanut butter and chocolate, sea salt and caramel, furikake and popcorn.

Add to this list chicken and lychee.

This Chinese dish comprises fried chicken pieces merged with a sauce made with canned lychee and their juices. A little bit of tomato and chili peppers, combined with the lychee's sweetness, create a dish that's on the sweet side with some kick.

I make the dish with onions and bell peppers, but you could substitute other vegetables that also add crunch.

If you're lucky enough to have fresh lychee, peel and seed them over a bowl to catch the juices. You'll need about 2 cups of fruit and ¾ cup juice.

CHICKEN WITH LYCHEE SAUCE
Serves 4

1½ pounds boneless, skinless chicken thighs, cut in bite-size pieces
Vegetable oil, for frying
½ cup cornstarch, for dusting
1 medium onion, cut in eighths
1 large red bell pepper, cut in 1-inch pieces
1 (20-ounce) can lychee, drained, with liquid reserved

Marinade
1 tablespoon minced ginger
1 tablespoon minced garlic
2 tablespoons soy sauce
1 teaspoon sesame oil
½ to 1 teaspoon red chili flakes

Sauce
¾ cup lychee juice from can

2 tablespoons ketchup
2 tablespoons oyster sauce
2 tablespoons shaoxing, Chinese rice wine (optional)
1 tablespoon cornstarch

Combine marinade ingredients. Pour over chicken pieces and let sit 20 minutes.

Fill heavy skillet or wok with oil to about ¾-inch deep. Heat over medium-high until a bit of cornstarch dropped into oil sizzles. Lightly dust chicken pieces in cornstarch and, one by one, carefully drop into oil. Work in batches; do not crowd pot. Fry until lightly brown on both sides, turning once, 1 to 2 minutes per side. Drain on paper towels.

Combine sauce ingredients except cornstarch.

Pour out all but 1 tablespoon oil from skillet. Keeping heat at medium-high, add onions and stir-fry until softened. Add red peppers; stir-fry 1 minute. Add lychee; toss until heated through, then add ½ cup of the sauce. Lower heat and let simmer uncovered until peppers soften.

Add 1 tablespoon cornstarch to remaining sauce, stirring well to dissolve. Pour into skillet and stir to thicken sauce.

Place chicken, vegetables, and lychee in serving dish; cover with sauce.

Mochiko chicken takes wing with this recipe from a 1973 cookbook called *What's Cooking at Waialua?* printed by the Waialua Sugar Co. in celebration of its 75th anniversary.

The recipe is pretty basic: equal parts mochiko, sugar, and cornstarch, plus soy sauce and eggs. The wings soak in that mixture overnight, then are dredged in more mochiko and cornstarch, and fried. If you wanted you could add minced garlic.

The proportions, though, the technique and perhaps the application to wings makes them special, delicious, nicely seasoned, and very crisp.

I suggest you do your frying in a wide, shallow skillet. It's easier to keep the oil temperature stable and lets you fry more wings at a time than a deeper pot.

The cookbook attributed the recipe to a June Hirayama. Thanks, June.

WAIALUA CHICKEN WINGS

Serves 4 as a main dish

3 pounds chicken wings, tips removed
Vegetable oil, for frying

Marinade
2 tablespoons chopped green onion
¼ cup sugar
5 tablespoons soy sauce
1 tablespoon salt
¼ cup cornstarch
¼ cup mochiko
2 eggs

Coating
½ cup cornstarch
½ cup mochiko

Combine marinade ingredients, beating in the eggs. Pour over chicken wings and let marinate overnight.

Heat oil in wide, shallow skillet to 350°F. Combine coating ingredients. Remove chicken from marinade; dredge in coating, shaking off any excess. Fry about 5 minutes, until golden (test one piece by cutting to bone to check for doneness). Shake off excess oil and drain on paper towels.

Catfish are the water critters of choice at 3660 on the Rise. Catfish Tempura with Ponzu Sauce was one of the original dishes created by Chef Russell Siu for his Waiʻalae restaurant and remains a favorite on the menu.

"People who don't really like catfish or fishy fish, they like that dish," he said. "We have people calling in all the time to reserve catfish for the night."

The key is a thin batter made with tempura flour and ice water, with egg yolk to produce the yellow color. The chef suggests using an electric wok for frying because it allows for better temperature control than cooking on the stove.

A final tip: Serve the sauce UNDER the fish. Otherwise, it will make the fish soggy.

Update: A version of this dish with furikake remains on the menu at Siu's second restaurant, Kakaʻako Kitchen.

3660 CATFISH TEMPURA
WITH PONZU SAUCE
Serves 4

4 (8-ounce) catfish fillets
Salt and pepper to taste
½ cup flour
vegetable oil, for frying

Tempura Batter
1 egg yolk
4 cups water
2 cups tempura flour

Sauce
¼ cup sugar
¼ cup sake
½ cup soy sauce
1 cup mirin
1 teaspoon grated ginger
2 tablespoons prepared ponzu sauce

To make sauce: Combine first four ingredients in a saucepan and bring to a boil. Cool, then add ginger and ponzu. Set aside.

To make batter: Whip egg yolk into water, then slowly add mixture to tempura flour until you have 3 cups of batter. You will not need all the water. Batter should be like a thin pancake batter and slightly lumpy. Do not over mix. Lumps will be absorbed into the batter.

Season fish with salt and pepper, then dredge in flour. Shake off excess flour and dip in tempura batter.

Heat oil to 350°F. Use enough oil so that fillets will float. Fry fish about 10 minutes, until golden and cooked through. Spoon sauce onto plate and top with fish.

Douglas Tom and I have been recipe testing via e-mail, our aim being Hou See Soong, a Chinese stir-fry made with dried oysters that's served spooned onto lettuce leaves.

Douglas said he hadn't seen the dish on a menu in 20 or 30 years. This is apparently a dish from another generation; you won't find it in contemporary cookbooks. But I did find a few recipes in a cookbook first printed in 1941 and sent those to Douglas.

He started there, consulted friends who remembered the dish, dug deep into his own memory and came up with one version. This is the result of both our efforts. It's not difficult or fancy, but the oysters give the dish an intriguing smoky flavor. And the lettuce-leaf wrap makes it fun to eat.

Note: Dried oysters are sold in Chinatown markets in several grades. I used a medium grade that sells for $7 to $8 per half-pound bag.

HOU SEE SOONG
Serves 4

4 ounces dried oysters
1 tablespoon vegetable oil
½-inch piece ginger, peeled and minced
½ pound ground pork
2 large dried shiitake mushrooms, soaked, finely diced
¼ cup minced bamboo shoots
¼ cup minced water chestnuts
¼ cup minced celery
¼ cup minced green onion
Cilantro leaves, for garnish
⅛ to ¼ cup crushed roasted peanuts (optional)
Lettuce leaves
Hoisin sauce, for dipping (optional)

Sauce
1 tablespoon soy sauce
2 tablespoons sherry
2 tablespoons soaking water from oysters
1 tablespoon sugar

Soak oysters in water at least 6 hours, or overnight. Drain well, reserving 2 tablespoons of soaking water. Remove any stringy parts, then dice.

Combine sauce ingredients; set aside.

Heat oil in a large skillet or wok. Add ginger and stir-fry until fragrant. Add pork and stir-fry until no longer pink. Stir in diced oysters, then mushrooms, bamboo shoots, water chestnuts, celery, and green onion. Add sauce; stir-fry 2 minutes. Taste and adjust seasonings.

Serve on a platter, garnished with cilantro and peanuts, with lettuce on the side. Spoon mixture onto a lettuce leaf, roll up, and dip in hoisin.

L inguine with Clams is the most-requested dish at Harpo's Pasta & Piz-za in Kapahulu and has become a Harpo's signature. A half portion has seven large Manila clams, a full portion twelve, and always fresh.

Owner Mike Trombetta says he wants to load the plate with clams, "then charge what you have to charge without gouging."

Update: In 2000 Harpo's celebrated its 25th anniversary with several locations on O'ahu. One is left, on Bishop Street downtown.

HARPO'S LINGUINE WITH CLAMS
Serves 1

¼ cup diced shallots
2½ tablespoons minced fresh garlic
¾ cup fresh button mushrooms
4 teaspoons butter (divided)
¼ cup dry vermouth
½ cup clam juice
⅛ cup chopped fresh parsley
1 pinch EACH salt, fresh ground pepper and chopped fresh
   thyme
12 fresh Manila clams
¼ cup sliced green onions
⅛ cup grated Parmesan cheese
12 ounces cooked linguine

Sauté shallots, garlic, and mushrooms in 3 teaspoons butter until mushrooms brown on the edges. Add vermouth and simmer until evaporated. Add clam juice, parsley, salt, pepper, and thyme. Bring to a boil for 15 seconds.

Reduce heat; add clams and onions and cover. Once clams open, remove them to a plate.

Add cheese and remaining teaspoon butter to the pan. Toss until butter is melted, then add pasta and toss.

Serve with clams on top of the linguine. Garnished with a parsley sprig and more green onions.

Kasuzuke is the lesser-known cousin of misozuke, as in Misozuke Butterfish, that well-loved, slightly sweet pairing of fish and miso.

Kasuzuke incorporates sake kasu—or sake lees, a byproduct of the sake-making process. It's a light, pasty substance that resembles miso, and if it doesn't sound all that attractive, remember that miso is really fermented soy bean paste.

It is frequently used in Japan with fish, especially salmon, as well as in soups and to make pickles. It is more subtle than miso and so requires more sugar and salt to bring out the flavor. That flavor is vaguely boozy, by the way—remember, the root ingredient here is sake, which is more potent in terms of alcohol than wine. Do not serve to someone who is sensitive or allergic to alcohol.

Find sake kasu at Japanese markets, refrigerated near the miso. This recipe can be made with the salmon in place of the gindara, or butterfish.

GINDARA KASUZUKE
Serves 4

4 (6-ounce) butterfish fillets

Marinade
6 ounces (²/₃ cup) sake kasu
1 ounce (2 tablespoons) mirin
8 ounces (1 cup) water
2 teaspoons light soy sauce
¼ teaspoon white pepper
5 tablespoons sugar
2 teaspoons salt
2 teaspoons grated ginger

Combine marinade ingredients well. Marinate fish, refrigerated, at least 18 hours.
Broil fillets 8 to 10 minutes.

The Olive Tree, just outside of Kahala Mall, is Savas Mojarrad's third Hawai'i restaurant experience. He started about thirty years ago with the Mad Greek, a nightclub-restaurant on Cooke Street. Many years later came the first Olive Tree, on Ala Moana Boulevard.

He ran each for a number of years, then took six or eight years off.

"I take kind of big vacations and I say, 'I'll never do it again,'" Savas explains. "Then it takes four or five years and I forget and then I do it again."

These souvlaki, or kebabs, made with fish, chicken, or lamb, come skewered with onions and are served with tzatziki, a yogurt sauce. For the fish version Savad uses fresh 'ahi, ono, mahimahi, nairagi, or other white fish.

OLIVE TREE FRESH FISH SOUVLAKI
Serves 4

2 pounds fresh white fish fillet
1 onion, cut in pieces ½ inch wide by 1½ inches long

Marinade
¼ cup vegetable oil or light olive oil
2 tablespoons lemon juice
4 cloves garlic, crushed
1 teaspoon oregano, crushed
1 teaspoon fresh dill or ½ teaspoon dry
½ teaspoon salt
Pinch black pepper

Remove bloodline from the fish and cut into pieces ½-inch thick and 1-inch square.

Combine marinade ingredients and pour over fish and onions. Refrigerate at least 2 hours. Place on bamboo skewers, alternating onion and fish pieces. Broil or grill to desired doneness.

TZATZIKI (YOGURT SAUCE)

Makes about 4 cups

4 cups plain yogurt
1 Japanese cucumber, chopped, skin on
4 cloves garlic, crushed
¼ cup chopped fresh mint, or 1 teaspoon dry
1 tablespoon chopped fresh dill, or 1 teaspoon dry
1 tablespoon vinegar
Salt and pepper to taste

Line a strainer with a piece of cheesecloth and suspend over a bowl. Pour yogurt over cheesecloth. Excess liquid in the yogurt will drain into the bowl. Refrigerate overnight or until yogurt is reduced by one-third.

Combine strained yogurt with remaining ingredients and refrigerate at least 6 hours.

Niitsuke refers to a reduced sauce of sugar and soy sauce that is served with fish. With strong-flavored fish such as butterfish, water is traditionally used in the sauce, but with more delicate fish such as onaga or flounder, the water may be mixed with dashi to add to the taste.

The traditional formula is 4 parts water (or water-dashi in equal amounts) to 1 part soy sauce and 1 part sugar. For those who prefer a stronger brew, the ratio can be reduced to 3–1–1.

This recipe calls for covering the fish loosely with foil, rather than a pot lid. This allows for steam to escape so the sauce reduces, without drying the fish.

BUTTERFISH NIITSUKE
Serves 2

1 pound butterfish steaks
1 cup water
¼ cup sugar
¼ cup soy sauce
5 to 6 slices of ginger, ⅛-inch thick
3 stalks green onion, in 2-inch lengths

Cut fish into large chunks, leaving skin on. Place fish on the bottom of a shallow pan, in a single layer.

Combine water, sugar, soy sauce, and ginger, mixing until sugar is dissolved. Add to pot. Fish should be ¾ covered. Cover loosely with foil.

Bring to a boil. Continue cooking rapidly about 2 minutes, until sauce begins to reduce. Remove foil and continue cooking until fish is done, another 3 minutes. As the sauce reduces, spoon liquid over the fish so it doesn't dry out. Add green onions in the last minute of cooking.

Fish will be very soft. Remove carefully. Garnish with julienned ginger and Japanese chili pepper, if desired.

Variation: Lay slices of konbu in the pot beneath the fish to add flavor and keep the fish from sticking. Gobo (burdock root) or tofu may also be added to the pot.

" About thirty years ago I was able to purchase from a local Chinese restaurant a dish called Butterfly Shrimp," a reader wrote. "The shrimp was butterflied and wrapped in bacon and coated with egg and fried." She included a P.S.: "There were no snow peas with this dish."

I could see the reason for the postscript as soon as I started searching. Lots of recipes exist for Chinese butterflied shrimp and snow peas, but no bacon. In fact, the use of bacon makes this dish seem out of place as a classically Chinese dish. The recipes I did find were on a website for Australian cooking, which could be a clue to its origin.

BUTTERFLY SHRIMP WITH BACON
Serves 4

24 large shrimp
8 slices bacon, cut in thirds
¼ cup vegetable oil
2 eggs, beaten

Sauce
3 tablespoons EACH sugar, rice vinegar, and ketchup
¼ teaspoon salt
½ cup water
1 teaspoon minced garlic
2 teaspoons cornstarch, dissolved in 2 tablespoons cold water

Shell and devein shrimp, leaving tails intact. Butterfly by making a slice down back, not quite all the way through. Spread halves apart and press flat. Wrap a piece of bacon around each shrimp.

Heat wok or skillet over medium heat, then add oil. Dip shrimp into beaten egg and place in wok. Fry 2 minutes, or until golden brown. Turn and fry another 2 minutes. Drain on paper towels, leaving oil in wok.

To make sauce: Reheat wok. Combine sugar, vinegar, ketchup, salt, water, and garlic. Add to oil in wok. Bring to boil and stir in cornstarch slurry to thicken. Serve with shrimp.

Hari Kojima has gone from local television, but memories of his *Let's Go Fishing* and *Hari's Kitchen* shows from the 1980s and 90s remain strong.

His molded crab dip is easy to assemble, using the creamy trio of cream cheese, mayonnaise, and cream of mushroom soup. A bit of unflavored gelatin is added and it goes into a mold. Let it set in the refrigerator, then unmold, surround it with crackers, and make it the centerpiece of a finger-food table. It makes enough for a party.

One tip: The most time-consuming part is grating a cup of celery. If you've never done this before (I hadn't), the advantage is that it gets rid of all the strings. The disadvantage is that celery is so watery and porous that the stalks sort of collapse against the grater and you've got to watch out for your knuckles. Lots of water comes out, so be sure to squeeze it dry before adding it to the crab mixture.

Also, obviously you get the best results with the best quality crabmeat. You'll find a big price difference between the usual canned stuff and premium chunky grades. The cheap stuff does produce a good dip, but if you want a hefty crab flavor to stand up to all that cream-cheesiness, you'll have to put up the bucks.

Update: Hari Kojima died in 2011 at age 66.

HARI KOJIMA'S KING CRAB DIP

8 ounces cream cheese
1 (14.5-ounce) can cream of mushroom soup
1 cup mayonnaise
1 (8-ounce) can crabmeat, drained well
1 cup grated celery, with excess water squeezed out
7 stalks green onion, minced
Salt and pepper, to taste
1 package unflavored gelatin
2 tablespoons warm water

Melt cream cheese in sauce pan over low heat. Add soup and mayonnaise and stir until smooth. Remove from heat. (Or combine all 3 in large bowl and microwave 1 to 2 minutes.)

Stir in crab, celery, green onion, salt, and pepper.

Dissolve gelatin in water and stir into crab mixture. Place in greased mold. Chill overnight.

Unmold onto platter and serve with crackers.

mediterranean couscous salad

parc cafe fried tofu salad

MEATLESS MEALS

A chapter like this might be titled "Salads and Sides," but I'm making a point here: Meat-free dishes belong in the center of the plate, not just in the position of accompaniments.

Most of the recipes in this collection would stand as main dishes—substantial salads such as the Mediterranean Couscous or the hearty portobellini mushrooms. Even the basic macaroni salad has potential as a main dish if you pile on more raw vegetables.

For non-vegetarians, nutritionists say it's a good idea to go without meat for a meal or two every week. These dishes will help accomplish that.

For diehard carnivores, there's something for you here, too. Many of these dishes can be topped with a bit of animal protein, and on balance you'll still be getting a good amount of vegetable nutrition.

The Honolulu Country Club serves these marinated and broiled mush-rooms as part of a salad. The recipe has become one of my favorites when I'm out to win friends and influence people. I don't even bother with any salad, I just serve up the mushrooms, sliced.

A couple of notes: This may seem like a lot of marinade, but I found in trying out the recipe that it does take a lot to coat the surface area of these large mushrooms, and they soak up a lot. Marinating in a sealable plastic bag is the best way to assure even coating, since the mushrooms are so bulky. Finally, try to get all the minced garlic from the marinade onto mushrooms—during broiling, the garlic turns nice and toasty.

BROILED PORTOBELLINI
Serves 4

6 portobellini mushrooms or 2 to 3 portobello mushrooms, depending on size

Marinade
¾ cup extra virgin olive oil
¾ cup balsamic vinegar
2 tablespoons chopped garlic
2 teaspoons fresh thyme

Whisk marinade ingredients together. Place mushrooms and marinade in a plastic bag, seal and shake to coat mushrooms. Marinate 10 minutes.

Broil mushrooms 5 to 8 minutes per side, until cooked through. Cool, then slice. Mushrooms may also be grilled.

One of the world's great snack foods is edamame—soy beans. And a great, handy way to get them is frozen, already shelled, cooked, and ready to eat by the handful.

But you can fancy them up, too.

Eric Leterc, executive chef at the Pacific Beach Hotel, created this salad in collaboration with Alan Wong when the two chefs opened Wong's Hawai'i Regional Cuisine Marketplace. The salad became a mainstay of the deli case. When Leterc moved to the hotel, he brought the salad along.

Update: Eric Leterc is now chef at the Pacific Club.

FRESH SOY BEAN SALAD
WITH FETA CHEESE
Serves 2

6 ounces shelled soy beans
2 ounces diced feta cheese
1 tablespoon minced shallots
1 tablespoon diced red tomatoes
1 tablespoon diced yellow tomatoes
1 tablespoon finely sliced basil
1 teaspoon cracked coriander seed
2 tablespoons balsamic vinegar
¼ cup olive oil
Pinch black sesame seeds
Juice from half a lime
Salt and pepper to taste

Combine all ingredients. Adjust seasonings, balancing the lime, vinegar, and olive oil. Let sit about 20 minutes to allow flavors to blend.

T hese soy-based dishes are regular on the buffet line at the Parc Cafe—standouts even amid a sea of menu choices. They are among the most popular items and have been on the line for years.

The Parc Cafe, in the Waikiki Parc Hotel, offers a number of themed buffets through the week.

Update: The Parc Hotel closed in 2016 for renovations.

PARC CAFE FRIED TOFU SALAD
Serves 4 to 6

1 pound block firm tofu
Vegetable oil for frying
¼ medium round onion, thinly sliced
2 stalks green onion, thinly sliced
1 teaspoon toasted sesame seeds

Dressing
⅓ cup oyster sauce
1 tablespoon sesame oil
1 tablespoon soy sauce
½ teaspoon sugar
⅛ teaspoon chili pepper flakes (optional)

Cut tofu in ¾-inch cubes, dry on paper towel, then fry in oil heated to 350°F, until light golden brown. Drain on another paper towel.

Whisk together all the dressing ingredients. Toss with tofu and add round onion slices. Garnish with green onions and sesame seeds.

PARC CAFE CHARBROILED
EGGPLANT WITH MISO DRESSING
Serves 4 to 6

2 round eggplants, in ½-inch slices
⅓ cup olive oil
Salt and pepper to taste

Miso Dressing
⅓ cup white miso
⅓ cup mirin
2 tablespoons rice vinegar
¼ teaspoon minced garlic
¼ teaspoon minced ginger
1 tablespoon olive oil
1 tablespoon sugar

Brush eggplant with oil and season with salt and pepper. Charbroil, or broil on top rack of oven, until golden brown and tender.

Whisk together dressing ingredients, adding a little water if too thick. Ladle dressing over eggplant; garnish with green onions if desired.

Hiroshi Fukui of Hiroshi Eurasion Tapas was one of the first friends I made when I started writing about food—lucky for me. His advice has saved me all kinds of time researching Japanese cooking. (Once he even called another restaurant for me and got a recipe out of a cook who didn't speak English.)

Hiroshi's food is not traditionally Japanese, though. It is a merger of Japanese and European techniques—in foodie circles it's called Eurasian—but he does it in a way that's never fussy or silly.

Whatever name eventually falls to this cuisine—new wave, neo-Japanese, Japanese-with-a-twist—it is a limitless source of challenge and opportunity.

"If you think about it, the variations of Japanese and European flavors, there's no end to it," Hiroshi says. "You can keep creating."

Update: Hiroshi left the restaurant that bore his name in 2013, eventually taking a position as vice president for Rainbow Drive-In. He now runs that busy site as well as Hawai'i's Favorite Kitchens next door, continuing his more upscale cooking as a private chef.

DASHI
Makes 6 cups

6 cups cold water
1 (6-inch) piece dashi konbu (dried kelp), rinsed quickly in cold water
1 cup katsuobushi (dried bonito flakes)

Place water and konbu in a pot over high heat. Remove konbu just before water comes to a boil. Stir in katsuobushi and turn off heat. Let sit 2 minutes, until katsuobushi settles in bottom of pan.

Skim and strain stock.

HIROSHI'S KILAUEA TOFU
Serves 4

1 block tofu
1 cup katakuriko (potato starch)
Vegetable oil for frying

Sauce
18 ounces (2¼ cups) dashi (previous page)
3 ounces (6 tablespoons) mirin
3 ounces (6 tablespoons) light soy sauce
1 teaspoon sugar
1 teaspoon Thai chili sauce

3 teaspoons katakuriko (potato starch), dissolved in 2 teaspoons water
½ cup sliced mushrooms, mix of oyster and shiitake
¼ cup sliced bell peppers, mix of green, red, yellow

Garnish
Katsuobushi (bonito flakes)
Diced chives
Grated ginger

Cut tofu into 8 blocks. Drain well on paper towels.

Dredge tofu pieces lightly in potato starch. Heat oil to 350°F and fry tofu until light brown and crispy.

To make Sauce: Combine dashi, mirin, soy sauce, sugar, and chili sauce in a saucepan and bring to a boil. Stir in katakuriko slurry, adding it a little at a time and stirring as sauce thickens. Once sauce is thick enough to coat a spoon, add mushrooms and bell peppers.

Serve tofu with sauce, topped with garnishes.

Note: If making the sauce ahead, leave out vegetables. Sauce may be kept, refrigerated, up to 2 days. Bring to a boil and add vegetables.

I don't know if I'll ever understand macaroni salad—how it came to be, why it's called a "salad," why so many people seem to need a recipe to make one. It's mayonnaise and macaroni, people!

I say this so you understand I am not a connoisseur, if there even is such a thing when it comes to mac salad. When I make it I go light on the mayo and heavy on the add-in veggies, especially watercress.

These two versions—from Diner's in Kalihi and Rainbow Drive-In—have very different techniques.

The Diner's trick is to grate the onions very, very fine. They'll actually be soupy. Add the liquid and all to the salad. This allows the flavor to really blend into the noodles. It's a good trick to remember for potato salad, too.

At Rainbow the cooked macaroni sits in water for a while, then drains overnight. Once dressed, the salad is chilled for another night to get the flavors just right.

Both use Best Foods mayonnaise.

Update: The last restaurant in the Diner's chain, the Waimalu location, closed on New Year's Eve 2016. Rainbow Drive-In is still going strong.

DINER'S MACARONI SALAD
Serves 10

1 pound macaroni, cooked
1 to 2 cups mayonnaise (Best Foods preferred)
1 cup watercress, in ½-inch pieces
1 cup shredded carrots
¼ cup very finely grated onion
½ cup finely diced celery
¼ teaspoon salt
⅛ teaspoon pepper

Combine all ingredients, mix well and refrigerate at least one hour to allow flavors to mix and mellow.

RAINBOW DRIVE-IN
MACARONI SALAD
Serves 20

8 to 10 cups water
1 pound uncooked elbow macaroni
1 teaspoon salt
½ teaspoon black pepper
½ teaspoon MSG (optional)
2¼ cups mayonnaise (Best Foods preferred)

Bring water to boil, add macaroni, boil 30 to 35 minutes on medium-high. Remove pot from heat; add 3 cups cold water and set aside 10 minutes. Drain and rinse in cold water to remove starch. Let drain in colander at least 3 hours but best overnight.

Combine remaining ingredients. Add to macaroni and mix. Refrigerate overnight; serve cold.

The scalloped potato dish served on the brunch menu at Orchids at the Halekulani is really a masterpiece of simplicity: just five ingredients— and two of them are salt and pepper. There's no thickener (such as the flour found in most scalloped potato recipes), so there's not even any stirring involved.

Why is it special? All the cheese that goes over the top has a lot to do with it. Plus the dish is chilled overnight, which allows everything to set up nicely before you slice it, reheat, and serve.

My test version came out of the fridge firm and as easy to slice as a cake. Once reheated, the cream and cheese softened just a bit, into a puddle of yum.

ORCHIDS SCALLOPED
POTATO GRATIN
Serves 10

8 Yukon Gold potatoes (about 3 pounds), peeled and thinly
   sliced
Salt and white pepper, to taste
1 quart (4 cups) heavy cream
2 cups grated Parmesan cheese

Heat oven to 375°F.

Layer potatoes in baking pan, sprinkling with salt and pepper between layers. Pour cream over the top, making sure all the potatoes are covered. Cover pan with foil and bake 45 minutes.

Remove foil and bake another 10 minutes, until top is golden brown.

Top with cheese and return to oven until cheese browns.

Chill overnight. Cut in square portions and reheat.

Jicama, if you have not yet made its acquaintance, is a vegetable you could learn to love, despite its tough, rugged exterior and toxic relatives.

Nicknamed "chop suey yam," jicama has crossed the globe and is commonly found in Chinese stir-fries and Mexican slaws. It also shows up naked—simply cut into sticks to serve on veggie platters. And fried. And tossed into salads, sandwiches, and stews.

A large, hard globe, jicama needs to be peeled—a sharp knife works better than a vegetable peeler—and sliced. That's it. The flavor is mild and the texture crisp. It tends to absorb the flavors of whatever you cook it with, making it a good companion.

Beware the relatives, though. The edible part of the jicama plant is the root. The leaves, stem, peel, flowers, and seeds all contain a toxin.

It's generally sold trimmed down to the friendly root, though. Look for jicama in Asian markets or in Chinatown. Your mainstream grocery stores might not have it.

JICAMA STIR-FRY
Serves 6

2 tablespoons vegetable oil
2 large cloves garlic, minced
Thumb-size piece ginger, peeled and minced
1 small onion, thinly sliced (about 1 cup)
½ pound jicama, peeled and cut in thin matchsticks (about 2 cups)
¼ cup chicken broth, divided
1 red bell pepper, thinly sliced (about 1 cup)
¼ pound green beans, cut on bias (about 1 cup)
2 tablespoons oyster sauce
Sliced green onions, for garnish

Heat oil in large skillet or wok over medium-high. Add garlic and ginger; stir until fragrant. Add onions; stir 1 minute. Add jicama; stir, then add half the chicken broth. Stir-fry 2 minutes, then add bell pepper and beans. Stir, then add remaining broth. Stir-fry until vegetables are crisp-tender, 3 to 4 minutes. Stir in oyster sauce. Serve topped with green onion.

JICAMA SLAW
Serves 6

¾ pound jicama, peeled and shredded (about 4 cups)

¾ pound red cabbage, shredded (about 3 cups)

1 teaspoon salt

1 cup finely sliced sweet onion

1 small sweet apple, cored and thinly sliced (1 cup)

1 chili pepper, seeded and minced (optional)

¼ cup minced cilantro leaves

Dressing
¼ cup lime juice

1 tablespoon sugar

1 tablespoon vegetable oil

Combine jicama and cabbage in colander; toss with salt. Let sit 10 minutes to draw out excess liquid. Press to squeeze out liquid. Place in large serving bowl.

Add onion, apple, chili pepper (if using), and cilantro; toss.

Whisk dressing ingredients together; pour over slaw in bowl and toss (the amount of dressing will seem inadequate, but more liquid will be drawn out of the vegetables). Refrigerate and let flavors merge at least an hour. Toss, taste, and adjust seasonings just before serving (a little soy or fish sauce can be added).

"To cook Indian, it takes a lot of patience," says chef Ronald Thomas Minezes.

Indian food typically involves marinating, followed by long, slow cooking and reduction of sauces, Minezes says. It can take three hours to make a single dish.

Minezes is corporate chef in Mumbai, India, for Sodexo, an international food-service company that provides cafeteria services in facilities such as schools and hospitals. He visited the University of Hawaii at Manoa as part of Sodexo's Global Chef program, which sort of stirs the pot, sending chefs around the world to bring knowledge of international cuisines to local cooks and diners.

Most of the recipes he brought with him were far too complex for home cooking, but these side dishes just require a small dash of ambition.

If you're used to buying a bottle of a spice and taking years to use it up, a teaspoon at a time, these recipes are going to seem alarming in the quantities of spices they call for. If you're worried the flavors might be too intense, start with half the amounts of spices (especially the chili powder), taste, and adjust.

RAJMAH MASALA
(KIDNEY BEAN CURRY)
Serves 10

1 pound dry red kidney beans
2 quarts water
¾ cup sunflower or canola oil
1½ cups chopped onions
1½ tablespoons minced ginger
1 tablespoon minced garlic
3 tablespoons red chili powder
¼ cup ground coriander
1½ teaspoons salt
1¼ cups diced tomatoes
1 tablespoon garam masala powder
Cilantro leaves, for garnish

Soak beans in pot of water overnight.

Place pot over medium-high heat; bring to boil. Lower heat and simmer beans until fully cooked, 45 to 60 minutes. Add water if needed as beans cook. Drain; set aside.

Heat oil in skillet over medium-high. Add onions and sauté until browned. Mix in ginger and garlic. Add chili powder, coriander, salt, and tomatoes. Cook until oil begins to seep out of mixture, 7 to 8 minutes.

Add beans. Cook 10 minutes more. Mixture should be thick, but add water if it's too thick.

Stir in garam masala. Taste and add more salt if needed. Serve garnished with cilantro leaves.

ALOO GOBHI
(CAULIFLOWER AND POTATOES)
Serves 10

3 pounds potatoes, peeled and cut in chunks
1¾ pounds cauliflower, broken into florets (about 7½ cups)
3 tablespoons salt
¼ cup ground turmeric
2½ tablespoons sunflower or canola oil
3½ tablespoons cumin seeds
2 cups chopped onion
2¼ cups chopped tomatoes
¼ cup red chili powder
¼ cup ground coriander
1 cup water
Cilantro leaves, for garnish

Bring pot of water to boil; add potatoes and parboil. Remove and drain.

Add cauliflower, salt, and turmeric to same pot of boiling water; parboil cauliflower. Drain.

Heat oil in skillet over medium-high. Add potatoes and fry until browned. Drain on paper towel-lined plate to remove excess oil.

Add cumin seeds to skillet; sauté until they begin to pop. Add onions and brown. Stir in tomatoes. Let simmer 8 to 10 minutes.

Add chili and coriander, then potatoes and cauliflower. Stir to mix well, adding water as needed to thin slightly. Serve garnished with cilantro leaves. Sprinkle with more salt if needed.

Couscous is a teeny, tiny type of pasta—so tiny that it looks like a grain and has a texture something like a grain, which makes for very interesting salads.

This dish is served on the buffet at Naupaka Terrace in the 'Ihilani Resort and Spa at Ko 'Olina, where executive sous-chef Jason Kin says it is a good buffet partner. "This is a very refreshing salad that complements all types of cuisines."

That it is and that it does. My test batch was consumed with gusto by the family, paired one night with ham and another with corn dogs (although this is probably not what he meant by "all types of cuisines").

Update: The 'Ihilani has become a Four Seasons Resort. Naupaka Terrace is now called La Hiki Kitchen.

MEDITERRANEAN
COUSCOUS SALAD
Serves 6

½ cup diced zucchini, ¼-inch pieces
½ cup diced red bell pepper, ¼-inch pieces
½ cup diced tomato, ¼-inch pieces
¼ cup minced parsley
¼ cup minced green onion
¼ cup raisins
1 tablespoon lemon juice
1 tablespoon olive oil

Couscous
1 tablespoon olive oil
½ tablespoon ground cumin
1 teaspoon turmeric
1 (10-ounce) box plain couscous
½ teaspoon salt
¼ teaspoon pepper
3 cups chicken stock

To prepare couscous: Heat olive oil in pot over medium heat. Add cumin and tumeric; stir to toast spices. Add couscous; stir to coat. Season with salt and pepper. Add stock and bring to simmer. Turn off heat and cover pot. Let rest 15 minutes, until liquid is absorbed. Fluff with fork; remove from stove and let cool.

Combine vegetables, raisins, lemon juice, and olive oil in serving bowl. Toss well. Stir in cooled couscous. Taste and adjust seasoning. Refrigerate until ready to serve.

People generally like coleslaw because it's creamy, tasty, and such a good match for barbecue, fried chicken, and other foods that set off the happy meters in our minds.

But coleslaw comes with baggage, specifically two suitcases: fat and sugar. That's largely thanks to the mayonnaise and the fact that KFC has taught us to like our coleslaw sweet.

So in pursuit of the greater good, I spent some time working on a creamy coleslaw without mayonnaise. Most recipes that tackle this recommend plain yogurt as a substitute, and this does work as a base. Rice vinegar (smoother than lemon juice), mustard, and pepper round out the dressing, with a squirt of soy sauce for umami, and because this is Hawai'i. To make up somewhat for a lack of sugar, shredded apples go into the mix.

The dish is relatively low in all our nutritional enemies. So if your gold standard for coleslaw is the KFC version and you find this slaw lacking in sweetness, go ahead and sprinkle on some sugar. You'll still come out ahead.

NO-MAYO CREAMY
COLESLAW WITH APPLES
Serves 10

6 cups shredded head cabbage
2 cups shredded red cabbage or radicchio
1 small carrot, shredded
1 small red onion, shredded
2 teaspoons kosher salt or 1 teaspoon table salt
1 small sweet apple (such as Fuji or Envy), very thinly sliced
    (about 1 cup)
½ cup chopped cilantro

Dressing
1 cup plain Greek yogurt
2 tablespoons rice vinegar
½ teaspoon Dijon mustard
½ teaspoon pepper
1 teaspoon soy sauce

Toss cabbages, carrot, and onion with salt and place in large colander in sink. Let sit 1 to 4 hours to draw excess water from vegetables. Toss again and press lightly to remove more water. (If you are on a low-sodium diet, rinse vegetables to remove salt; press out water and pat dry with paper towels.) You will start with about 10 cups of shredded vegetables; after excess water is drained you'll have about 8 cups. Place in large bowl with apples and cilantro.

Whisk dressing ingredients together. Thin slightly with water if dressing is too thick. Toss with slaw mixture. Chill. The flavors in this salad are mild, and chilling mutes them even more, so taste and adjust seasonings before serving.

Variations: The red cabbage and carrot may be substituted with any crisp, colorful vegetable, such as bell peppers, raw beets, broccoli, or a mix. Red onion may be replaced by a sweet, white onion. Total volume of these vegetables and the onion should be 3 to 4 cups.

If you saw a lady in the produce aisle last weekend spending way too much time looking at bags of carrots, that was me.

I was trying to pick the one that had the most carrots of the size and shape of hot dogs. Not too fat, not too thin and not too tapered.

My objective was to make Carrot Dogs. I was skeptical, but the ingredients were cheap and the process was simple. I didn't think I would get anything that actually tasted like a hot dog—at best I'd get some good cooked carrots; at worst, bad cooked carrots.

In the end, my fake hot dog was pretty good. Did it taste like a real one? Not at all. But I figured, what the heck. I put it on a piece of bread, squirted it with ketchup and mustard and ... dang, what a surprise. Light, tasty, and just a bit hot-doggish. It was either the power of positive thinking or the magic of ketchup and mustard.

Try these at your next barbecue. Those who don't eat hot dogs will appreciate the effort. Others might appreciate the novelty.

CARROT DOGS
Serves 4

4 carrots, hot dog size, peeled, ends trimmed
4 hot dog buns, toasted
Garnishes, as desired: mustard, ketchup, diced or grilled onions, relish, sauerkraut, chili

Marinade
¼ cup soy sauce
¼ cup water
2 tablespoons seasoned rice vinegar (see note)
1 teaspoon garlic powder
1 to 2 drops liquid smoke
¼ teaspoon pepper

Bring a pot of water to boil. Add carrots and reduce heat. Let simmer 10 to 15 minutes, until carrots can be pierced with a fork but are still firm (very important that they not get mushy). Drain.

Combine marinade ingredients and stir to dissolve garlic powder. Pour over carrots. Let marinate 2 to 4 hours.

Grill carrots or sauté in a skillet, brushing with marinade until nicely browned, about 10 minutes.

Serve in toasted buns; garnish as desired. Serves 4.

Note: Seasoned rice vinegar is a sweetened Japanese vinegar used for making sushi rice and is easy to find in the Asian aisle of supermarkets. Or substitute 2 tablespoons rice vinegar and 1 tablespoon sugar.

R aw black rice is reminiscent of midnight, but when cooked it turns an intense purple and the cooking water gives off a violet hue. That color is its badge of good nutrition: Black rice has more protein, fiber, and antioxidants than white, brown, or red rice, and is loaded with vitamins and minerals. It's the only rice with anthocyanin, a specific beneficial antioxidant stored in the outer hull which is responsible for the grain's dark color.

During China's Ching and Ming dynasties only the emperor could eat black rice. Thus its alternate name: forbidden rice. It was thought to ensure longevity and good health in China's heads of state.

All of this would count for nothing if the rice didn't also make a good meal.

It's got more heft and a nice chewiness compared with white rice, and a mild, nutty taste. This warm rice salad with a lemon vinaigrette includes garbanzo beans and corn, which are popular at my house, but you could substitute equal amounts of any bean or vegetable. Bell peppers, cucumbers, tomatoes … all fine. Chard or kale in place of the spinach … all fine.

Make sure one component is crunchy and one a little sweet to balance out the flavor and texture. In this recipe apples satisfy both those needs, but you could also throw in dried fruits or nuts.

WARM BLACK RICE SALAD
WITH GARBANZOS
Serves 4

2 cups water
1 cup black rice
1 teaspoon salt
3 ounces spinach leaves (about 1 cup, packed)
1 cup corn kernels
½ cup garbanzo beans
1 cup diced sweet apple
1 cup chopped green onion

Dressing
¼ cup lemon juice
½ cup olive oil
½ teaspoon chili flakes

Bring water to boil in small pot. Add rice and salt; reduce heat to simmer. Cover and let cook 20 to 30 minutes, stirring occasionally, until water is mostly absorbed. Rice should be tender but not too soft.

Stir spinach into pot and let cook a few more minutes until spinach is wilted. Turn off heat; cover and let sit a few minutes.

Combine dressing ingredients in jar and shake well.

Empty pot of rice into serving bowl; add corn, beans, apples, and onions. Stir in dressing; toss well.

halekulani macadamia nut cream pie

liliko'i cake

SWEET ENDINGS

People are on diets. People are full. Yet somehow dessert is rarely a hard sell. The butter and sugar help, of course. Chocolate often lends an assist as well. And whipped cream.

From a few cookies on a plate to a spectacular tiered cake, a good dessert is temptation personified.

That diet doesn't stand a chance.

This cookie is made with arare. It is quite good, especially right out of the oven. I ate five before I remembered my diet.

A couple of notes: This seems like a lot of butter, and the dough is quite greasy, but it's right. Also, you can crush the arare very fine or go for more of a coarse crush. I'd go for a fine crush if you expect to keep the cookies around for several days. Larger chunks of arare tend to get too chewy and stick to the teeth (you know how arare gets after just a little time in humid air).

ARARE COOKIES
Makes about 3 dozen cookies

1½ cups butter, softened
1 cup firmly packed brown sugar
1½ teaspoons baking soda
2 teaspoon vanilla extract
1 tablespoon soy sauce
1 egg
3 cups flour
1¾ cups Rice Krispies®
1½ cups arare (mochi crunch), crushed

Heat oven to 350°F.

Cream softened butter and brown sugar until light and fluffy. Add baking soda, vanilla, soy sauce, and egg and beat well. Add flour and mix until just well-blended. Add Rice Krispies® and crushed mochi crunch and mix well.

Roll into 1-inch balls and place 2 inches apart on cookie sheet, flatten slightly. Bake 8 to 10 minutes or until golden.

Susy Kawamoto has shared many of her cookie recipes with newspaper readers, including this one for mochiko cookies, a good match in taste and texture for the popular Keith's mochiko shortbread, although they don't bake up into the same familiar little mounds.

Kawamoto says you can experiment with mochiko—Japanese rice flour—in adapting your own favorite recipes. Substitute mochiko for a portion of the flour in the recipe, but never more than 1 cup mochiko to 1 cup of flour.

MOCHIKO BUTTER COOKIES
Makes about 2 dozen

½ pound butter, softened
¾ cup sugar
1 teaspoon baking soda
2 teaspoons vanilla
1½ cups flour
½ cup mochiko
1 cup chopped macadamia nuts (optional)

Heat oven to 350°F.

Cream butter and sugar until light and fluffy, 5 to 8 minutes. Add baking soda and vanilla. Mix well. Add flour, mochiko, and chopped nuts, if using; blend well. Drop by rounded teaspoonfuls onto cookie sheet and bake 15 to 20 minutes or until slightly golden.

The usual coconut pie is a creamy thing, which makes this Coconut Macaroon Pie something unique for the dessert table.

It was served at the Honolulu Community College bakeshop a couple decades ago, back when HCC had a bakeshop.

The pie uses macaroon coconut, which is NOT the same as shredded baker's coconut that you'll find at the grocery store. Macaroon coconut is dried and comes in tiny flakes. If you can't find it at your market, try a health-food store.

COCONUT MACAROON PIE
Makes 1 (8-inch) pie

1 cup sugar
2 tablespoons plus ½ teaspoon cornstarch
2 cups water
⅛ teaspoon almond extract
2 cups macaroon coconut
1 teaspoon butter, in pieces

Prepared double crust for an 8-inch pie

Heat oven to 350°F.

Combine sugar and cornstarch. Add water and almond extract. Cook over medium heat until mixture comes to a boil. Remove from heat and stir in coconut. Cool to room temperature.

Pour filling into pie crust and dab butter around filling. Cover with top crust and seal. Make slits in the top crust or a single hole in the center to vent steam. Bake 40 minutes, or until crust is golden or filling can be seen bubbling through the center hole.

Prunes get a bad rap. It's that name: "Prune" just sounds like squishy, wrinkled, old-lady food. Or, worse, a stool-softener. Prune-makers have even come up with the new name of "dried plum" to get past all that.

This recipe turned up in response to a request from a reader whose mother always made her a prune cake for her birthday. She wanted to do the same for her kids. The recipe is from *Seasons of Baking 2*, a self-published cookbook from Henry Shun, a retired commercial baker.

Henry says the cake is reminiscent of those once served as wedding favors. If you can get past that fear of prunes, this is a moist and flavorful, not-too-sweet dessert. And if you can't get past it, Henry suggests trying the cake with other dried fruits, such as raisins, dates, figs, or cranberries.

HAPPY BIRTHDAY PRUNE CAKE
Makes one square cake

1½ cups plus 2 tablespoons cake flour
2 tablespoons bread flour (see note)
1 cup sugar
½ teaspoon salt
1 teaspoon baking soda
2 teaspoons baking powder
¾ cup vegetable oil
3 large or 4 medium eggs
1 teaspoon vanilla
2 teaspoons lemon juice
3 ounces chopped prunes (¾ cup loosely packed)
½ cup plus 2 teaspoons milk
Pinch cinnamon

Heat oven to 365°F. Line bottom of a 8- or 9-inch square cake pan with parchment paper. Do not grease.

Sift together flours, sugar, salt, baking soda, and baking powder.

Combine oil, eggs, vanilla, lemon juice, and prunes in a mixing bowl. Beat at low speed 3 minutes. Add dry ingredients and beat 4 minutes. Add milk and cinnamon, scrape sides of bowl and beat 1 more minute. Pour batter into pan. If desired, sprinkle a few more chopped prunes over top of cake.

Place pan on a cookie sheet (to keep bottom from darkening). Bake on center rack 30 to 35 minutes, or until cake is firm and leaves no indentation when touched. Cool, remove from pan and wrap in plastic wrap. Let "age" one day for best flavor.

Note: All-purpose flour may be used in place of bread flour.

Toffee is a hard candy made with butter and sugar, often paired with chocolate and nuts for a winning combination of softness, richness, and crunch (think of a Health candy bar).

A Chocolate Coffee-Toffee Pie replicates the flavor, if not the texture, through a creamy filling of butter, sugar, and melted chocolate, with coffee stirred in for good measure.

One warning: This crust can be very difficult to dig out of the pie pan, so grease very well. You could also simplify matters by substituting a standard graham cracker crust.

Or, dispense with a crust altogether—the filling is so good it could be served alone as a mousse.

CHOCOLATE COFFEE-TOFFEE PIE

Makes 1 (9-inch) pie

Crust
1 cup flour
½ cup (1 stick) butter, softened
¼ cup light brown sugar, lightly packed
1 ounce (1 square) unsweetened chocolate, grated
1 teaspoon vanilla extract
2 tablespoons water
¾ cup finely chopped walnuts or pecans

Filling
½ cup (1 stick) butter, softened
¾ cup sugar
2 teaspoons powdered instant coffee
1 ounce (1 square) unsweetened chocolate, melted
2 eggs

Topping

2 cups whipping cream

¼ cup powdered sugar

2 tablespoons instant coffee or 2 tablespoons coffee liqueur (Kahlua, Tia Maria, etc.)

Heat oven to 375°F. Grease a 9-inch pie pan very well, or line bottom with baking parchment.

To make crust: Combine flour, butter, brown sugar, and chocolate using a pastry cutter or by hand. Add vanilla, water, and nuts. Use hands to mix dough until it holds together in a ball. Add a few drops more water if necessary. Press dough into pie pan by hand. Prick all over with a fork. Bake 15 minutes. Cool.

To make filling: Beat butter on high speed until fluffy. Gradually beat in sugar. Beat in instant coffee and melted chocolate. Add 1 egg; beat on high speed 5 minutes. Add second egg and beat 5 more minutes. Spread filling in cooled pie shell. Cover and refrigerate several hours, until firm.

To make topping: Beat cream at high speed until peaks form. Stir in sugar and coffee and beat until stiff. Spread over chilled pie and refrigerate 1 hour before serving.

Brian Jahnke, manager of the Waioli Tea Room, has a memory that goes way, way back—and a recipe collection to match.

This proved to be good news for a reader who had been nursing a craving for the date bars that she enjoyed at the tea room—she guesses thirty years ago. "I've been haunted by this recipe for years," she wrote.

It's easy to see why, once you've baked up a batch. These bars are soft, chewy, and just sweet enough.

If you've been to the Waioli Tea Room lately, note that these are not the bars currently on the menu; they come from a generation ago.

It's a simple recipe. My only caution is to resist the urge to cut into them too soon. They are very soft right out of the oven and need time to set up.

Update: The Waioli Tea Room closed in 2014.

WAIOLI TEA ROOM DATE BARS
Makes 12 bars

Filling
2 cups chopped dates
½ cup brown sugar
1 cup water
1 tablespoon flour
4 teaspoons vanilla

Crust
1¼ cups flour, sifted
1 teaspoon baking soda
3 cups old-fashioned rolled oats
1 cup brown sugar
1 cup butter, melted

To make filling: Combine all ingredients except vanilla in a saucepan and simmer over medium-low heat until dates are soft and mixture thickens, 3 to 4 minutes. Cool. Stir in vanilla.

Heat oven to 350°F. Lightly grease an 8- or 9-inch baking pan.

To make crust: Combine flour, baking soda, oats, and sugar. Mix well. Add butter and stir to combine. Press half the crust mixture into the bottom of pan. Spread date filling evenly over bottom crust. Top with remaining crust and press gently into an even layer. Bake 35 to 40 minutes, until top is lightly toasted.

Cool completely before cutting.

The Chinese Tea Cookie—Kong Sui Ban—was an elusive recipe. I had requests on file dating to 2001. Finally three readers all turned up with family recipes.

All the recipes were similar, with basic ingredients save one: wong tong, or Chinese brown sugar. I got good results substituting regular brown sugar, but I like wong tong for the flavor and sense of tradition.

These cookies won't win any beauty contests—they're nondescript, tan discs—but the flavor is superior. Don't expect an exact duplicate of what you're used to buying in Chinatown (where they're sometimes sold as "tea cakes"), but the texture's a match and the taste is really, really close.

One baking note: these cookies are typically sold very large, three inches across or even more. You might want to make them smaller—better for munching.

CHINESE TEA COOKIES
Makes 20 large cookies

1 cup water
5 slabs (about 13 ounces) wong tong (Chinese brown sugar;
  see note)
½ cup white sugar
5½ cups flour
2 tablespoons baking powder
¼ cup honey
1 cup vegetable oil
2 eggs

Bring water to boil. Break wong tong into pieces and add to water. Stir to dissolve. Remove from heat and stir in white sugar to dissolve.

Whisk together flour and baking powder.

Combine honey and oil; beat in eggs. Add to flour mixture and stir to combine. Add sugar syrup and mix until smooth. Let rest 1 hour.

Heat oven to 350°F. Cover cookie sheets with baking parchment.

Scoop dough onto cookie sheets and press flat (about ½-inch thick). Cookies should be 3 inches wide for traditional size, but it's OK to make them smaller. Bake 12 to 15 minutes.

Cool slightly on cookie sheet, then move cookies to a rack.

Note: Wong tong is sold in blocks in most grocery stores in Chinatown. Or use 1½ cups brown sugar in place of wong tong.

A t a time of loss and sadness, you know what you need? Mochi cake. Beth An Nishijima of Nori's Saimin & Snacks in Hilo knows this by the amount of her Chocolate Mochi Cake ordered for funerals. "It goes well with tea and coffee."

It also goes well with water, or juice, or nothing. Chewier than a cake but not as fudgy as a brownie, a slice of mochi cake is "bouncy," as Nishijima describes it.

Nishijima has been making the cake for twenty-five years and demand has never faded. She still serves 100 pieces a day, much of it to visitors buying in bulk for omiyage.

Over the years, she's learned that her cake seems to have eternal life. People wrap it and refrigerate or freeze it, or sometimes mail it to relatives. A little microwaving and, "It's brand new, it tastes like you just made it. ... Warm it up and it gets bouncy again, and moist."

NORI'S CHOCOLATE MOCHI CAKE

Makes 2 loaves

4½ cups mochiko
4½ cups sugar
5 tablespoons cocoa powder
2 teaspoons baking powder
1 (13.5-ounce) can coconut milk
1 cup evaporated milk
5 eggs, beaten
1 tablespoon vanilla extract
1 stick butter, melted

Heat oven to 375°F. Grease two 5 x 9-inch loaf pans. Combine mochiko, sugar, cocoa powder, and baking powder. Mix well so baking powder is well distributed.

In a separate bowl combine coconut milk, evaporated milk, eggs, vanilla extract, and butter. Add to dry mixture and stir until batter is smooth. Pour batter into loaf pans and bake 75 to 90 minutes, until center does not jiggle at all.

Cool and cut into pieces with plastic knife.

The reason liliko'i is called passion fruit in English is that it is passionately awesome. OK, I made that up. But it is true that pure, fresh liliko'i is magical.

Just mix a little juice and powdered sugar into a thin sauce. Taste. You see? Tart, assertive, fragrant. A wallop of yum.

This recipe is based on one for a lemon pound cake. It can be made as a loaf, cupcakes, or with some adjustments, a 9 x13-inch sheet cake. But I like it best in loaf form, befitting its pound-cake origins.

This cake is fabulous, not due to my skill but because of the magical properties of liliko'i. I may have mentioned those before.

LILIKO'I CAKE

6 to 10 liliko'i, depending on size (passion fruit, see note)
2 sticks butter, softened
1 cup sugar
4 eggs
1 teaspoon vanilla extract
1½ cups flour
1 teaspoon baking powder
½ teaspoon salt

Cut liliko'i in half and scoop contents into colander or strainer set over a bowl. Let juice drain, stirring occasionally, 1 hour. Place remaining pulp (with seeds) in blender and purée. Strain through fine-mesh sieve, pressing with spoon to remove seeds. Discard seeds (some seeds will make it into the purée; this is OK, it will give the cake tiny black specks). You should have about ¼ cup purée; if not, add some juice. Save remaining juice for another use.

Heat oven to 350°F.

Grease a 9 x 4-inch loaf pan or a 9 x 9-inch cake pan, or place 18 paper cups in muffin pans.

Cream butter and sugar until fluffy. Beat in eggs one at a time. Add vanilla.

In another bowl, combine flour, baking powder and salt. Beat dry mixture gradually into creamed mixture. Add ¼ cup liliko'i purée. Batter should turn smooth and silky.

Pour into prepared pan or cupcake cups. Bake 60 minutes for loaf pan, 50 minutes for cake pan or 45 minutes for cupcakes, until a pick inserted into the center comes out clean. Do not over bake or cake will be dry.

Note: To make this cake in a standard 9 x 13-inch pan, increase recipe by 1½. Fresh liliko'i is sold at farmers markets and in Chinatown, or purée is sold at R. Field Wine Co. and ChefZone.

Τhis creamy pie is served on the buffet at Orchids at the Halekulani. It's exceptional, with a light, delicate filling and just enough toasty macnut flavor.

The recipe is somewhat involved, so I'm going to stop talking now, except to note that Orchids' chefs provided measurements by weight, and I've included approximations in cups and tablespoons. But weighing your ingredients will yield the most precise results.

HALEKULANI MACADAMIA NUT
CREAM PIE
Makes 1 (10-inch) pie

Crust
8 ounces (about 1¾ cups) flour
¼ teaspoon salt
¼ teaspoon sugar
4.8 ounces (about 9½ tablespoons) cold butter, cut in cubes
1.6 ounces (about 3 tablespoons) cold water

Filling
16 ounces (2 cups) whole milk, divided
1 ounce egg yolk (1 yolk from large egg)
1½ ounces (about ⅓ cup) cornstarch
¼ vanilla bean
4 ounces (½ cup) sugar
¾ ounce (1½ tablespoons) butter
½ cup macadamia nuts pieces, toasted, plus more for garnish
Whipped cream, for topping

To make crust: Heat oven to 350°F. Combine flour, salt, and sugar in a mixer with paddle attachment. Cut butter cubes into flour mixture until it breaks up into pea-size pieces. Mix in just enough water so dough comes together. Do not over mix. Chill overnight.

Roll dough out to about ¼-inch thick and fit into 10-inch pie pan. Trim excess dough and flute edges. Fill with pie weights if desired. Bake 30 minutes, until golden brown. Cool.

To make filling: Combine 4 ounces (½ cup) milk with egg yolk and cornstarch, stirring to make a slurry.

Pour remaining 12 ounces (1½ cups) milk into small pot. Cut open vanilla bean and scrape seeds into milk. Add sugar; bring mixture to boil. Add cornstarch slurry, whisking to avoid lumps. Stir in butter. Return to a boil, whisking continuously, and cook for about 1 more minute. Stir in nuts. Chill mixture.

Beat chilled filling to soften it, then pour into pie shell. Top with whipped cream and sprinkle with more toasted macadamia nuts.

A baked good that makes use of leftover Halloween candy is a fine a public service. It helps you get temptation out of the house in a form that other people will happily consume.

I'm not talking about popular candies—M&M's, Reese's Peanut Butter Cups, most chocolate bars—your kids probably ate all those already, and if not they're easy to get rid of as is. I'm talking about the lesser candies that can linger into the new year until you finally throw them out, or lie in wait until you eventually eat some in a moment of weakness.

For example, Whoppers.

Whoppers are balls of malted milk coated in chocolate. Not a traditional favorite as a candy, but they make great brownies.

Seriously, these were the chewiest brownies I've ever made, with a malted flavor that distinguished them from the usual chocolate.

WHOPPER BROWNIES
Makes 1 (9-inch) square pan

¾ cup malted milk powder (sold in supermarkets near the
chocolate milk mixes)
1 cup brown sugar, firmly packed
1½ cups flour
¼ teaspoon salt
½ teaspoon baking powder
3 large eggs
½ cup butter, slightly melted
1 teaspoon vanilla
1 cup Whopper candies, chopped (see note)

Heat oven to 350°F. Line a 9-inch square pan with baking parchment, letting paper extend over edges of pan.

Combine malted milk powder, sugar, flour, salt, and baking powder in large bowl.

In a separate bowl, beat eggs, butter, and vanilla until creamy. Add to bowl with malted milk mixture, stirring to make a smooth batter. Fold in Whoppers. Pour into prepared pan. Bake 30 to 40 minutes, until center is firm.

Place pan on rack and let cool slightly. Use edges of parchment to lift brownies from pan; let cool completely, then slice into squares.

Note: You'll need about 60 Whoppers. Those little trick-or-treat packs hold three each, so you'll need 20 packs. If your kids didn't collect that many, Whoppers are sold in boxes in most stores with candy aisles.

guava chiffon cake

toong mai

WORTH THE EFFORT

Most of the recipes printed in *By Request* are user-friendly, meaning they can be tackled by the average home cook. I try to avoid recipes with long lists of hard-to-find ingredients, complicated instructions, or those that call for special kitchen equipment.

I have made exceptions, however, for dishes so popular or so rewarding that the payoff is worth the effort.

The best way to tackle one of these: Read carefully and go slow.

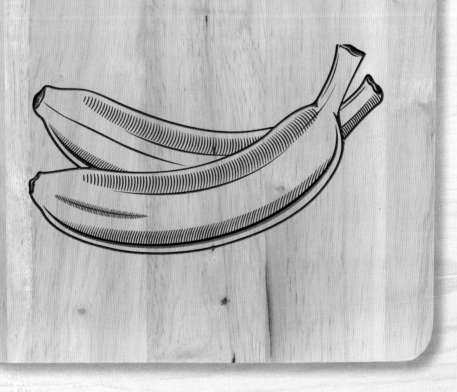

For years the Chicken Alice recipe for spicy Korean chicken wings was the No. 1 request sent to me and all my predecessors. Then in early 2005, a friend of mine recognized Alice Yang at her place of work, a bar called Club Star Palace, where she was the manager.

Alice Yang—better known as Chicken Alice—was famous in the 1980s and 90s for her wings, until the restaurant, on Kapiʻolani Boulevard just outside Ala Moana Center, closed in 1995.

Once I found her, Alice happily gave up the recipe, saying it was payback for the warmth that she'd received since moving here. "I give it away to state of Hawaiʻi people," she said. "I hope they like it."

The recipe is simple, but technique counts for a lot. By that I mean skillful deep-frying. Alice's wings are nice and crunchy on the outside, juicy and perfectly cooked inside. If you don't fry a lot, you'll probably have patchy results until you get the hang of it.

Update: Alice died in 2015 and a fan posted a message on the memorial website run by the funeral home: "RIP Alice," it read. "Your wings were the absolute bomb."

CHICKEN ALICE'S WINGS
Serves 12-15

5 pounds chicken wings
Vegetable oil for deep frying (Wesson brand preferred)

Batter
1/3 cup Parks Brand kim chee sauce
1 tablespoon minced garlic
2 tablespoons salt
2½ cups flour
2 cups water, or more, as needed

Rinse and dry chicken. Cut off and discard wing tips. Cut through joint to separate drummettes from other half of wing.

To make batter: Combine kim chee sauce, garlic, salt, and flour. Add water gradually, enough to make a thick batter.

Add chicken pieces to batter, mix well and marinate in refrigerator 2 to 3 hours.

Heat oil to 350°F. Deep-fry chicken pieces about 10 minutes, until chicken rises to surface and coating is deep brown.

Just about every restaurant has a dish or two that can't be removed from the menu because the customers won't allow it. At Ryan's Grill that would be the Cajun Chicken Fettuccini.

Chef Bill Bruhl says the recipe came from Paul Prudhomme's New Orleans restaurant years ago when Prudhomme trained several Ryan's chefs on Cajun seasonings and dishes. "It's an item I would never even think of removing from the menu."

The complexity of the dish is what makes it work, Bruhl says, specifically the blend of seven dry spices rubbed into the chicken.

RYAN'S GRILL
CAJUN CHICKEN FETTUCCINI
Serves 8

2 pounds chicken tenderloins, in 1 x 1-inch pieces
3 tablespoons Spice Blend (recipe follows)
½ pound unsalted butter
1½ pounds fettuccini, blanched al denté
Fresh grated Parmesan cheese, for garnish
Green onion curls, for garnish (see note)

Sauce

6 ounces (¾ cup) unsalted butter
⅓ medium onion, in ⅛-inch dice
3 whole garlic cloves
1½ tablespoons minced garlic
Scant 2 teaspoons thyme

1 heaping teaspoon cayenne
Scant teaspoon white pepper
Pinch black pepper
Scant ½ teaspoon dried basil
1¾ cups plus 2 tablespoons chicken stock
1½ tablespoons Worcestershire sauce
3 teaspoons hot sauce (such as Tabasco)
3 cups tomato sauce
1⅓ tablespoons sugar
⅓ bunch green onions, in ⅛-inch slices

To make sauce: Melt butter over medium-high heat. Add onions and whole garlic; sauté 5 minutes. Add minced garlic and dry seasonings. Cook until onions are dark brown.

Add stock, Worcestershire, and hot sauce. Bring to a rapid simmer and cook 20 minutes.

Add tomato sauce and return sauce to a simmer. Stir in sugar and green onions and continue to simmer for 1 hour.

To prepare pasta: Rub chicken pieces with Spice Blend.

Melt butter over medium heat. Add chicken and sauté until just cooked. Add sauce and cook 1½ to 2 minutes. Add pasta and toss to coat. Continue to sauté until sauce clings to pasta.

Serve in large dish, garnished with Parmesan and green onion curls.

Note: To make curls, slice green onion thinly on the bias. Soak in ice water; slices will curl.

Spice Blend
3 tablespoons kosher salt
1 tablespoon white pepper
1 tablespoon garlic powder
5 teaspoons cayenne pepper
3 teaspoons black pepper
3 teaspoons ground cumin
1½ teaspoons dried basil

Combine all ingredients and store in an airtight container.

Toong mai is a crunchy Chinese puffed-rice cake, sort of like Rice Krispy Treats, but better. It is a favorite of celebrations such as the Lunar New Year, but not often made in the home, for good reason.

The traditional method involves soaking and steaming the rice, drying it in the sun, then making it pop in a wok filled with hot sand.

I have never found anyone willing to show me how it's done, and such a project could not be carried out in a home kitchen anyway, so after much experimentation I came up with this method. It ain't easy.

Before you begin, check your equipment: You'll need a steamer, preferably the Chinese bamboo type, cheesecloth, a couple of small pots, a rolling pin, spatula, and a flat, wire-mesh strainer.

Also, check your schedule: Working straight through, this will take most of the day, on top of soaking the rice overnight. You can spread the work out over a couple of days, though.

And, check the weather: It's best not to attempt this on a humid or rainy day.

TOONG MAI

Serves 4 to 6

1 cup mochi rice (sweet, glutinous rice)
Vegetable oil for deep-frying
1 cup water
½ cup sugar
1 teaspoon vinegar
¼ cup dry-roasted peanuts, preferably unsalted

Cover rice in water and soak at least 3 hours or overnight.

Drain rice. Spread a layer of cheesecloth in the bottom of a steamer basket. Place rice in an even layer over cheesecloth. Cover and steam over boiling water 40 minutes, or until rice is soft. Cool.

Heat oven to 175°F. Spread rice evenly on a baking sheet (grains will be very sticky, but try to separate as much as possible). Bake 45 minutes. Every 15 minutes turn and separate rice so it dries evenly.

Turn off oven. Leave rice in oven 3 to 4 hours, until completely hard and dry.

Pour about 2 inches of oil into a small pot. Heat to 375°F.

Scoop a small amount of dried rice onto strainer and lower into hot oil. The rice will puff and rise. Use strainer to separate and turn rice grains. When rice just starts to color—in a few seconds—lift out with strainer, tapping the side of the pot to shake off excess oil. Drain on paper towels.

Working in small batches, puff the remaining rice. (Don't try to hurry the process by using a larger pot. The rice cooks quickly and will burn if you can't get it out of the pot fast enough.)

Break up any clumps of rice and immediately store in an airtight container. You should have about 4 cups. Discard oil. (If you're tired now, go to bed. Finish in the morning).

Bring water, sugar, and vinegar to a boil. Simmer until a thick syrup forms and mixture begins to turn light brown, about 30 minutes (240°F to 245°F on a candy thermometer, halfway between soft- and hard-ball).

When syrup is almost ready, combine puffed rice and peanuts in a large, lightly oiled bowl. Oil a spatula and a baking sheet. Pour syrup over rice and stir quickly, using spatula, so rice is evenly coated. Work quickly, as syrup cools and hardens quickly. Spread on baking sheet and form by hand into a ¾-inch thick layer. Press firmly with a rolling pin to compress to 1½-inch thickness, pushing in the edges as you go to maintain shape. Cool and cut.

Variations: Grated ginger and sesame seeds may be added to the puffed rice. You can also vary the amount of peanuts and experiment with more or less syrup, depending on how sweet or chewy you like it.

You have to dig to find Jackie Lau's Mexican roots—past her Chinese married name (Lau), past her German maiden name (Groth) to her mother's family name (Flores).

Lau was schooled in Mexican cooking by three generations of Flores women—her mother, grandmother, and great-grandmother—during her childhood in California's San Joaquin Valley.

Jackie, corporate chef for Roy Yamaguchi's Hawai'i restaurants, came up with this chile verde dish to contribute to a Fourth of July article in 2002, when I was looking for four special dishes representing America's mixed heritage. This is not a Roy's dish, but something personal for Jackie and I think it says a lot of both her sense of adventure and tradition.

Update: Jackie left Roy's in order to spend more time with her son in his last year of high school. She is now building a business as a consulting chef and selling her pastry creations.

CHILE VERDE WITH PIG FEET
Serves 10

¼ cup pork lard or vegetable oil
2 pounds pig feet, cut into sections
2 pounds diced pork butt
1 large onion, diced
3 cups chicken stock or broth
21 ounces Herdez brand salsa verde (see note)
2 jalapeños, diced
3 bay leaves
2 tablespoons dry oregano
5 cloves garlic, smashed
1 tablespoon peppercorns

Place pig feet in a pot of salted water and bring to a boil. Boil 5 minutes; drain and rinse. Repeat process once.

Heat lard or oil in a large pot. Brown diced pork and onion. Add pig feet to the pot along with all of the remaining ingredients. Simmer, covered, on medium heat, 2 hours. Stir occasionally, to prevent sticking. Remove cover and simmer another hour to allow liquid to reduce and flavor to intensify.

Debone pig's feet, if desired. Serve with fresh chopped cilantro, lime wedges, and hot fresh tortillas.

Note: Most supermarkets carry the Herdez brand in the Mexican food section. It comes in 7-ounce cans.

The republic of nachos is a free country.

As long as you have chips on the bottom, anything goes. Top them with beef, chicken, pork, fish, or lobster, even. Add veggies (fresh or pickled), beans, salsa (any flavor), chilies, cheese. Top with guacamole, sour cream, neither or both. Create fusion mixtures as they do at Cisco's Cantina in Kailua, where co-owner Greg Blotsky makes rather inspired nachos with kalua pig and pineapple salsa.

As for the provenance of this dish—it is only loosely Mexican, the way that chop suey or fortune cookies are Chinese. That is to say, Mexican in style, but invented north of the border, then adopted back in the supposed homeland.

To which we say, that's very nice. We'll take some anytime.

Update: Cisco's closed in 2009

CISCO'S NACHO GRANDE

Serves 6

6 cups tortilla chips
6 ounces kālua pig
1 small tomato, chopped
1 small onion, chopped
½ cup chopped olives
½ cup each shredded cheddar and jack cheeses
2 tablespoons sour cream
2 tablespoons guacamole

Roasted Pineapple Salsa

1 cup canned cubed pineapple, roughly chopped
2 tablespoons brown sugar
1 tablespoon vinegar
½ teaspoon red pepper flakes
2 tablespoon finely chopped red bell pepper
2 tablespoons roughly chopped cilantro

To make pineapple salsa: Combine all ingredients in a baking pan except cilantro. Broil until pineapple edges turn slightly brown, 15 to 20 minutes. Stir well; cool. Mix in cilantro. Refrigerate an hour before serving.

Heat oven to 350°F.

On a 12-inch oven-proof serving dish, layer the nacho ingredients in the order listed, except the sour cream and guacamole. Top with pineapple salsa. Bake until cheese melts, about 5 minutes.

Top with sour cream and guacamole. Serve immediately.

Arare has always come into my house ready-made. Just like, say, shoes. I understand it is theoretically possible to make your own shoes, but how? And why?

Same for arare—also known as mochi crunch or kaki mochi—that slightly salty, ever crunchy Japanese rice cracker. This snack food is certainly cheap enough to buy in large quantity, and its quality, mass-production aside, rarely seems an issue.

But I have found that for every edible substance there is a person who wants to make it from scratch. And somewhere, there is a recipe.

Arare is both fried and baked, first to get it light and puffy, second to bake on a sweet-salty glaze. That glaze is the trickiest part. It needs to be cooked on the stovetop just enough to thicken slightly. Cook too long and it'll be too thick to coat evenly. The coated arare goes in the oven and it's hard to judge doneness because the glaze makes it very dark from the start. Too little baking and your arare will be sticky and not quite crunchy. Bake too long and it'll taste burnt. You need to check an individual piece for that elusive state of "almost done." The glaze will be set, but the arare won't be quite crunchy—that comes when it completely cools.

Best solution: Glaze and bake in small batches until you have the baking time right for your oven. The good news is, even when burnt this arare tastes pretty good.

JAPANESE RICE CRACKERS

Makes about 100 rice crackers

¾ cup flour
¾ cup mochiko
1½ tablespoons sugar
1 tablespoon black sesame seeds
1 teaspoon baking powder
½ cup water
Vegetable oil for frying

Glaze
¼ cup corn syrup
¼ cup sugar
¼ cup soy sauce

Combine flour, mochiko, sugar, sesame seeds, baking powder, and water to make a smooth dough. Add a little more water if dough is too dry.

Flour work surface lightly with mochiko. Roll out dough in small batches. Dough must be very thin, almost paper-thin. Use a knife to cut into ½-inch squares.

Heat oil to 375°F.

Fry crackers in batches until golden brown on both sides. This will take just a few seconds. Remove with a slotted spoon or strainer, tapping the sides of the fryer to remove excess oil. Drain on paper towels.

Heat oven to 300°F. Place cooled rice crackers on a cookie sheet.

To make glaze: Combine corn syrup, sugar, and soy sauce in a pan and bring to boil over medium heat. Cook until sugar dissolves and mixture begins to thicken, about a minute. Do not overcook or the glaze will be difficult to spread.

Pour glaze over rice crackers and mix to coat evenly. Work quickly, as glaze will harden as it cools. Spread crackers into a single layer and separate pieces. Bake 15 to 20 minutes, until glaze is set and crackers are dry but not quite crisp. They will harden and get crispy as they cool. Do not overbake or glaze will burn.

Twice-Cooked Chicken was a menu specialty at A Little Bit of Saigon, a popular Vietnamese restaurant on Maunakea Street in Chinatown in the 1990s. The restaurant has closed but co-owner Minh Na Vu remembers the recipe, which she developed based on a dish called Coconut Chicken that is popular in Vietnam.

"When I was in Vietnam we used to go to restaurants to eat and my mother ordered that dish," Vu said. "I fell in love with that dish. I learned how to make it just cooking at home."

The chicken is marinated in a mixture that includes the juice from a fresh young coconut. A can of coconut water is a good substitute.

After marinating, the chicken pieces are fried—that's the first-cooked part—then simmered in the marinade, which cooks down to a sauce that coats the chicken—the twice-cooked part. The result is a slightly sweet dish flavored with garlic, shallots, and soy sauce.

A LITTLE BIT OF SAIGON
TWICE-COOKED CHICKEN
Serves 4

1 fresh chicken, about 3 pounds, preferably free-range or
   organic
Vegetable oil for frying

Marinade
1 head garlic
½ cup of shallots (about 8 pieces)
2 tablespoons sugar
2 tablespoons fish sauce
2 tablespoons soy sauce
1 teaspoon salt
1 teaspoon pepper
Juice from 1 fresh young coconut, or 1 (10-ounce) can plain
   coconut water

Wash chicken in salted water, pat dry. Cut into 8 large pieces (leave
bones in).

To make marinade: Coarsely chop garlic and shallots. Combine with
remaining ingredients except coconut juice. Mix chicken pieces with marinade; add enough coconut juice so chicken is covered. Refrigerate a maxi-
mum of 3 hours.

Remove chicken, reserving marinade. Set chicken on paper towels and
let air-dry 15 minutes.

Heat oil in sauté pan over medium heat. Fry chicken until golden, lower-
ing heat to prevent burning.

Remove chicken; discard oil. Return chicken to pan with reserved marinade. Cook slowly, turning chicken occasionally until done. Sauce should
thicken and coat chicken.

Cut chicken into smaller pieces. Serve topped with remaining sauce in
pan.

Early in her marriage, Joyce Fasi began a quest of many months to satisfy her husband, Frank, the future mayor of Honolulu.

The object was a perfect spaghetti with meat sauce. She cooked; he tasted. He called up memories of the spaghetti of his childhood; she cooked again. Eventually he gave the recipe his approval.

The hearty tomato sauce includes a couple of pork chops and chicken thighs simmered until they basically fall apart and become one with the sauce. It is flavored heavily with fennel and anise seeds, "so it has a particular flavor that other sauces don't have," Fasi said.

The meatballs are huge things, made with lean ground beef, Romano cheese, onions, and parsley flakes.

Now in her late 70s, Fasi no longer cooks, leaving that to her children.

JOYCE FASI'S
SPAGHETTI AND MEATBALLS
Serves at least 12

1 (29-ounce) can tomato puree
2 (30-ounce) cans whole tomatoes, crushed by hand
2 quarts water
3 to 4 cloves garlic, crushed
1 tablespoon dried oregano
2 to 3 tablespoons Italian seasoning
1 to 2 tablespoons anise seeds
½ tablespoon fennel seeds
1 teaspoon red pepper flakes
1 to 2 bay leaves
¼ cup olive oil
2 bone-in pork chops
2 bone-in chicken thighs, skin removed
1 beef soup bone (optional)
Pinch baking soda
Salt and pepper, to taste
3 pounds dry spaghetti, cooked according to package directions

Meatballs
2 pounds lean ground beef
4 slices stale bread, torn in small pieces, moistened with water
  if very dry
½ teaspoon garlic salt
1 tablespoon parsley flakes
1 cup finely diced onion
4 eggs, beaten
½ cup grated Romano cheese
Salt and pepper, to taste

Combine tomato purée, tomatoes and their juices, water, garlic, and spices in large pot. Bring to boil then reduce to simmer.

Heat oil in skillet. Add pork chops and brown, then add to pot. Brown chicken thighs and add to pot with oil from skillet. Add soup bone, if using, and a pinch of baking soda to help cut tartness of tomatoes. Cover and let simmer on very low heat, 3 to 4 hours, tasting frequently to adjust seasonings with salt, pepper, and spices. Sauce should taste of anise (a licorice-like flavor).

To make meatballs: Heat oven to 350°F. Combine ingredients in large bowl and mix lightly by hand. Form into 24 meatballs, about 2 inches in diameter. Place on rimmed baking sheet and add water to about ¼-inch deep. Bake 15 minutes, or until cooked through.

When chicken and pork are very tender, remove bones and soup bone. Shred meat and return to pot. Gently add meatballs. Serve over cooked spaghetti.

A restaurant could be gone, but its best desserts are never forgotten. Such is the case with the Banana Mac-Nut Praline Tart from the Kahala Moon, which closed in 1998.

Chef/owner Kelvin Ro's tart is like a banana pie with a caramelized filling and a streusel-type topping.

Use ripe bananas, Ro says, the type with brown spots on the skin. "Half-ripe bananas don't do it for me," he says.

Also critical: "Pre-cook" the bananas by marinating them in a pineapple mixture before baking. "You want the banana to start absorbing the acid so it breaks down and it'll be one smooth consistency through the whole thing. The sauce won't penetrate through the whole banana unless you marinate it first."

The three-part recipe may look complicated, but Ro's step-by-step instructions break it down into common-sense pieces. As a bonus, run through it and you'll learn some professional tricks, such as letting the dough sit several hours so the gluten relaxes and the crust is tender—then, after rolling it out, putting the crust in the freezer briefly to firm it up.

Update: Kelvin Ro, now develops curriculum and plans special events for the culinary program at Kapi'olani Community College. In 2001 he opened Diamond Head Grill & Bakery on Monsarrat Avenue.

KAHALA MOON
BANANA MAC-NUT PRALINE TART

Orange Crust
2 cups sifted flour
1 teaspoon salt
1/3 cup chilled, unsalted butter
1/3 cup vegetable shortening
1 teaspoon orange zest
2 tablespoons powdered sugar
5 tablespoons ice water

Topping
½ cup chilled butter
½ cup flour
1 cup coarsely ground uncooked oatmeal (grind whole oats in
    food processor or blender)
½ teaspoon salt
½ cup brown sugar
¼ cup chopped macadamia nuts
2 tablespoons white sugar

Banana Filling
5 cups ripened bananas
½ cup canned crushed pineapple
¼ cup pineapple juice
¼ cup butter
½ cup brown sugar
3 tablespoons fresh-squeezed orange juice
1 teaspoon cinnamon
½ teaspoon nutmeg
1 teaspoon vanilla extract
¼ teaspoon salt
2 tablespoons flour

To make crust: Sift flour a second time with salt. Add remaining ingredients, except water, and mix until pea-sized granules form. Sprinkle water over dough and mix until dough forms a ball (may not need all 5 tablespoons). Refrigerate at least 12 hours to let gluten relax for a delicate pastry crust.

Roll out dough and place in a 10-inch spring-form tart pan or 2 (8-inch) pie pans. Place in freezer for 20 minutes to allow dough to cool and firm up again.

To make topping: Melt butter and add remaining ingredients, except white sugar. Mix thoroughly and chill at least 2 hours.

To make filling: Combine bananas, pineapple, and pineapple juice; let sit 10 minutes.

In a saucepan, melt butter then mix in brown sugar and orange juice until sugar dissolves. Do not boil or sugar will crystallize. Combine with bananas and remaining ingredients, adding flour last. Pour into chilled crust.

Heat oven to 350°F. Sprinkle topping over tart then sprinkle white sugar over all. Bake 40 to 50 minutes, until crust is baked and filling is set. Serve with vanilla ice cream and blueberries.

The Royal Hawaiian's haupia cake is as pretty in pink as the hotel that it represents.

The cake itself is a white chiffon, but it's layered with pink haupia, covered in pink-tinged whipped cream, and dusted with pink coconut flakes. Hello Kitty, this dessert's for you.

The professional version comes in dainty 4- and 6-inch sizes. This recipe has been scaled for a larger layer cake better suited to making at home.

ROYAL HAWAIIAN
PINK HAUPIA CAKE
Makes 1 (4-layer) cake

8 ounces (about 1¾ cups) cake flour
6 ounces (about ¾ cup) sugar
¾ tablespoon baking powder
4 ounces (½ cup) vegetable oil
4 ounces (about 5 large yolks) egg yolks
5½ ounces water

Meringue
8 ounces egg whites (from 7 large eggs)
4 ounces (½ cup) sugar

Haupia filling
1 (12-ounce) can coconut milk
4 to 6 tablespoons sugar
6 tablespoons cornstarch dissolved in ¾ cup water
3 to 4 drops red or pink food coloring

Topping
1 quart heavy whipping cream
6 ounces (¾ cup) sugar
Red or pink food coloring
Sweetened coconut flakes

Heat oven to 350°F. Lightly grease 2 (8-inch) baking pans (9-inch pans work, too). Line bottoms with parchment if desired.

Sift together cake flour, sugar, and baking powder; set aside.

In separate bowl, whisk together oil, egg yolks, and water; gradually add to dry ingredients, continuing to whisk until a smooth batter is created.

To make meringue: Whip egg whites until foamy then gradually sprinkle in sugar. Whip until stiff peaks form.

Gently fold batter into meringue, stirring until no streaks of white remain. Pour into prepared pans and bake 30 to 40 minutes, until a pick inserted into the center comes out clean. Let cool on rack.

To make haupia filling: Combine coconut milk and sugar in pot; bring to a boil. Gradually whisk in cornstarch-water slurry. Mixture will thicken quickly. Add food coloring to create a pink color, and continue whisking as mixture bubbles for 3 to 5 minutes. Pour into separate container and let cool completely.

To make topping: Whip cream with sugar to form medium peaks. Add food coloring to create a pastel pink. Set aside.

Color coconut flakes with more food coloring.

Remove cake from pans and cut each 8-inch round into 2 equal layers, for a total of 4 layers (see tip below).

Put cooled haupia in mixing bowl and beat until creamy.

Place 1 cake layer on serving plate. Top with a layer of haupia. Continue with more layers of cake and haupia to make 4 layers.

Cover the cake with pink whipped cream and sprinkle with coconut flakes.

Tip: It's easier to cut cake layers in half horizontally if you freeze the cake first. This makes it less crumbly and easier to handle. Wrap cooled layers in plastic wrap, then freeze for a few hours or overnight. To cut the layers, first let the cakes thaw slightly. Use a long serrated knife to cut each cake in half horizontally. If you don't trust your eye, measure the halfway point with a ruler and mark it at several spots around the cake with toothpicks, to guide your knife.

The guava chiffon cake was born shortly after Herbert and Sue Matsuba opened Dee Lite Bakery on Mokauea Street in 1959. The Matsubas called the cake Guava Delite and it took off.

The Matsubas retired in 1990 and sold the bakery and their recipes to Saint-Germain America, which continues to produce them. Many other local bakeries have their own versions.

I was never able to get the Dee Lite recipe, but I do have a good one.

GUAVA CHIFFON CAKE

Makes 1 large cake

5 egg yolks (using large eggs)
½ cup vegetable oil
½ cup water
¾ cup guava juice concentrate, thawed, undiluted
2 teaspoons vanilla
2¾ cups cake flour
⅔ cup sugar
4 teaspoons baking powder
1 teaspoon salt
2 to 3 drops red food coloring
2 to 3 cups whipped cream

Meringue
6 egg whites
½ teaspoon cream of tartar
½ cup sugar

Topping
2 tablespoons cornstarch
½ cup water
Pinch salt
12-ounce can guava juice (or use concentrate left over from
    cake batter, adding water to make ¾ cup juice)
1 teaspoon lemon juice
1 slightly beaten egg yolk
1 tablespoon butter
2 to 3 drops red food coloring (optional)

Heat oven to 325°F and lightly grease bottom of an 11 x 13-inch pan (see note).

Separate 6 eggs. Place 5 yolks in mixing bowl, set aside 1 for topping, place whites in separate mixing bowl for meringue.

Lightly beat 5 yolks. Add oil, water, guava juice, and vanilla. Set aside.

In separate bowl, sift together cake flour, sugar, baking powder, and salt. Make a well in center; add egg yolk mixture. Beat with a spoon until smooth. Stir in food coloring. Set aside.

To make meringue: Beat egg whites with cream of tartar until soft peaks form. Gradually beat in ½ cup sugar until stiff.

Gently fold batter into meringue until no white streaks remain. Pour into pan. Bake 35 to 40 minutes, until a pick inserted in the center comes out clean. Remove from oven and cool on a rack.

Loosen sides and remove cake to serving plate. Cake may be frosted as is or cut in half and assembled as a layer cake. Refrigerate cake while preparing topping.

To make topping: Mix cornstarch with water in small saucepan, stirring to dissolve lumps. Add salt, guava, lemon juices, and egg yolk. Cook over medium-low heat until thick, stirring occasionally, 5 to 10 minutes. (Mixture will thicken more as it cools, but if it seems too thin, combine another tablespoon cornstarch with water and slowly add more to saucepan.) Remove from heat and add butter. For a deeper pink, stir in food coloring. Let cool slightly, but spread while still warm and soft.

Frost cake with whipped cream, then gently spread topping over whipped cream, leaving a ½-inch border. If making a layer cake, spread topping evenly over bottom layer, reserving ¼ cup for top of cake. Place second layer on top layer; refrigerate 1 hour to firm up cake. Frost sides and top with whipped cream, then spread with remaining topping. Chill cake before serving.

Note: If you prefer a round cake, you will have enough batter for 3 round, 9-inch pans. Double topping recipe to make a 3-layer cake. Or fill 2 cake pans and use the extra batter to make cupcakes. Bake 9-inch cakes 25 to 30 minutes; cupcakes for 20 minutes.

INDEX

3660 Catfish Tempura with Ponzu
Sauce, 95

ABOUT THE AUTHOR

Betty Shimabukuro is the editor of the *Honolulu Star-Advertiser's* weekly food magazine, Crave. She has written the recipe column "By Request" for many years, beginning when it was part of the *Honolulu Star-Bulletin*.

Betty is a graduate of Kaiser High School and the University of Hawai'i journalism program. She's had a long career in newspaper work, spanning all manner of reporting and editing jobs, landing in food writing in 1998.

Until then her cooking training involved nothing more than a spotty apprenticeship with her mother, Betty Zane Shimabukuro, a home economist and a fine home cook. She has since improved on this base by working with some of Hawai'i's best chefs and home cooks.

Betty's husband, Rob, their three children—Justin, Christine, and Caleb—and their giant dog Jax are to be thanked for their role as test subjects in the experiments that are a part of a food writer's daily life.